Understanding the Bible as a Whole

Understanding the Bible as a Whole

An Accessible
Book-by-Book Guide
through the Scriptures

Sam Rainer

THOM S. RAINER, SERIES EDITOR

TYNDALE
MOMENTUM®

A Tyndale nonfiction imprint

Visit Tyndale online at tyndale.com.

Visit Tyndale Momentum online at tyndalemomentum.com.

Tyndale, Tyndale's quill logo, *Tyndale Momentum*, and the Tyndale Momentum logo are registered trademarks of Tyndale House Ministries. Tyndale Momentum is a nonfiction imprint of Tyndale House Publishers, Carol Stream, Illinois.

Understanding the Bible as a Whole: An Accessible Book-by-Book Guide through the Scriptures

Designed by Ron C. Kaufmann

All the examples and stories in this book are true. Names and some specific details have been modified to protect the privacy of the individuals involved.

For information about special discounts for bulk purchases, please contact Tyndale House Publishers at csresponse@tyndale.com, or call 1-855-277-9400.

Library of Congress Cataloging-in-Publication Data

A catalog record for this book is available from the Library of Congress.

ISBN 978-1-4964-6188-9

Printed in the United States of America

28	27	26	25	24	23	22
7	6	5	4	3	2	1

This book is dedicated to Margaret Bangston, our church grandmother. She loves her Bible. She lives her Bible. We can tell by the way she hugs our children.

Contents

INTRODUCTION

The Whole Bible for Your Whole Life

WHEN THE SUITCASES were opened in a crowded but secluded room in a Chinese village, everyone responded with excitement. They quickly reached for the contents. One by one, each person picked up one of the new books. Some kissed the cover. Others wept. Their joy was palpable. One young woman, her voice laden with emotion, spoke for everyone in the room: "This is what we needed most."

Then a hushed silence as—for the first time ever—they opened their own Bibles.

A missionary captured this scene on video in the 1980s, and a YouTube version of it went viral in 2014.[1] It inspired people around the world to cherish their Bibles.

As you read this book, my hope is that learning more about the Bible as a whole will stir a similar kind of awe in you, one that will make you eager to read your Bible each day. Because let's be honest—if someone brought a suitcase of Bibles to your church or small group, it probably wouldn't inspire a similar reaction.

Why is that?

Part of the challenge for many of us is that we struggle to

connect the dots between the whole of Scripture and the details of our own lives. We might cling to favorite verses when we're walking through valleys of defeat and death, but we've never experienced the big picture—the mountain peak of perspective and purpose. Which means we don't understand how the Bible as a whole connects to our lives—that we are part of an epic story as ancient as creation and as limitless as eternity. And yet it's my belief that we cannot understand our lives without understanding the Bible. "*All* Scripture is inspired by God," writes the apostle Paul, "and is useful to teach us what is true and to make us realize what is wrong in our lives. It corrects us when we are wrong and teaches us to do what is right. God uses it to prepare and equip his people to do *every* good work" (2 Timothy 3:16-17, italics added).

Every single word in the Bible is powerful, purposeful, and prescient. *All* of Scripture is for *every* part of our lives. But we sometimes fail to see the proverbial forest for the trees. We search the Bible thinking the details of God's plan for us must be buried in obscurity somewhere in the vastness of its pages. We might even fear we're missing God because we missed a tiny iota of nuance from the original Hebrew or Greek. But what if the opposite is actually the case? What if what we're missing is not the details but the big picture? What if our daily purpose, our next step, our discernment in the moment is plainly visible in a broader understanding of God's revelation in the Bible? What if our lives begin to make sense only when we grasp God's Word holistically—when we see the forest as well as the trees?

When the Chinese woman said, "This is what we needed the most," she spoke of the Bible as a whole. The people in the room wept together as they reverently held the entirety of God's Word. As we explore the grand themes of the Old and New Testaments, my prayer is that your excitement for the whole of God's Word will grow and you will begin to reach eagerly for your Bible each day. As you catch a larger vision of God's epic story, I hope you, too, will say with a full heart, "This is what I needed most."

Understanding the Bible Is Essential for Life

As you read each chapter, my hope is that you will gain more than just knowledge or information about the Bible. My aim is to inspire you to find God's purpose for your life as you understand the Bible as a whole. A life full of Scripture is always a full life.

The Bible is how we understand God's true character. Without God's Word, we wouldn't know how to interact with him. When we know God's character through the Bible, we are able to honor him by how we live our lives.

Our next steps in life are illuminated through Scripture. God's Word is "a lamp to guide [your] feet and a light for [your] path" (Psalm 119:105). As such, God's Word will assure you that you are living according to God's will. When you understand God's Word, you learn how to glorify your Creator and avoid sin. Not only will the Bible give you joy in living, but it will also protect you from the destructive nature of bad decisions. You can live a God-honoring life by diligently applying his Word (2 Timothy 2:15).

Understanding the Bible as a whole is worth the effort. Every word matters because every minute of your life matters. In Luke's Gospel, we're told that God numbers the hairs on our heads (Luke 12:7). God is always involved in every area of our lives.

The lesson is simple: God is active, caring, and present in your life at all times. He wants you to joyfully interact with him by reading, studying, and understanding the Bible. Your life matters, especially in the context of God's greater story. In the next section, I'll explain why.

God's Story of Redemption

The Bible is God's story of redemption—how he bought back his creation and the people who had fallen away from him. The first step in understanding the Bible as a whole is realizing that the biblical story is not so much *about* you as it is *for* you. The opening words of Genesis are "In the beginning *God* . . . ," not "In the beginning *you* . . ."

God creates. God speaks. God saves. He is not just *part* of creation or just a *power* in creation; he is *sovereign* over all creation. The story of the Bible is about God and his desire to redeem us. The apostle Paul tells us that God gave us the Bible for our "hope and encouragement" (Romans 15:4). The Bible is God's road map to hope.

The Bible reveals God's plan for redeeming his people. The story has ups and downs, failures and successes. It's not G-rated, and all the characters are flawed, with one exception—Jesus. God is holy and just, and his perfection demands judgment of sin. God is also love, and his mercy reaches out to us through grace. He desires to rescue us from ourselves. Paul emphasizes this when he writes that God is *for* us and not *against* us (Romans 8:31).

Throughout the Old Testament, a discernible pattern of sin and redemption emerges in the relationship between God and his people. God initiates a relationship with his wayward people, offering reconciliation. His people accept mercy and forgiveness but inevitably fall back into sin. God gives his people warnings. They do not listen. God gets their attention with judgment but also offers redemption. Once again, his people accept, only to fall away again. And the pattern repeats itself in generation after generation. The books of the Old Testament reveal this pattern through the law, through the historical works, through poetry, and through the prophets. By the time we get to the New

Testament, the sentiment is "We need the Messiah! We need a Savior!"

And that is the point. The Old Testament demonstrates our need for salvation, and the New Testament reveals the Savior—Jesus. The author of all things enters the story. Why? To redeem the people he loves. Through Christ, God saves and frees his people. And he then sends them out into the world as an army of gospel storytellers. The Bible is a true story of God's redemption of humanity, and the world needs to hear it. We have the Bible so we can share this remarkable story.

Salvation through Jesus Christ is the central theme of the Bible. Only Jesus can save us from our sins. The Bible contains the wonderful story of how Jesus' death and resurrection made redemption possible. At the center of human history stands a rugged wooden cross. What we believe about what happened on that cross determines our eternity. If we believe Jesus died for our sins, and that he offers us forgiveness by his grace and mercy, then we will spend eternity with God. Rejecting God's free offer of salvation separates us from him forever in hell. Accepting God's grace means repenting of (or turning from) our sins and accepting Jesus' sacrifice and resurrection as the means of our salvation. The theme of redemption is the unifying thread that runs throughout the entire Bible.

In fact, we cannot understand the story of redemption apart from the Bible. Some people try to understand God simply through nature and science. And God has certainly revealed himself in both. In Psalm 19:1, David writes, "The heavens proclaim the glory of God. The skies display his craftmanship." Similarly, the intricacies of science reveal the presence of a designer. Galileo, the great astronomer and father of the scientific method, believed God employed mathematics as the language of what Galileo called "the book of nature."² But although we can learn something about God *generally* through nature and science, it is only through the Bible that we gain insight into what God wants us to know about him *personally*. Only through God's Word can we learn how to have a relationship with him.

When we see things in the world that are complex and intricate, we can point to the presence of a designer. Motor vehicles are engineered and built. Sculptures are planned and chiseled. Restaurant meals are prepped and plated. We see evidence of the designer in any of these items, but we cannot claim to know the designer as a result. It's different with God. The divine Designer not only created the entire world for us to enjoy, but he also wanted us to know him and to have a relationship with him. God made that relationship possible by sending his Son, Jesus. And the Bible tells us the story of how Jesus is the hope of salvation. The Bible is the how-to book of hope.

God's Truth Is Eternal

How do we know the Bible is true? This question is fundamentally important. The Bible makes this claim of itself: "Every word of God proves true" (Proverbs 30:5). If the Bible were false, then God himself would be false. If we take the position that God is false, we are placing ourselves in authority over him by picking and choosing our own truth. But if we're picking and choosing, how do we know we're right, especially given that we're obviously not perfect or infallible? In order for there to be truth, there must be something absolute that establishes truth. The Bible is God's absolute truth revealed to us.

Another way to affirm the truth of the Bible is to consider what Jesus believed and taught about Scripture. One example is recorded in John 10, where Jesus is in the middle of a tense situation near the end of his public ministry. It is winter in Jerusalem—cold and rainy. He is walking through a section of the Jewish Temple known as Solomon's Colonnade when a group of people surrounds him and asks, "If you are the Messiah, tell us plainly." In other words, "Are you God?"

Jesus responds, "I have already told you, and you don't believe me." He goes on to explain, "The proof is the work I do in my Father's name," and then he summarizes by declaring, "The Father and I are one."

At this point, the crowd picks up rocks to stone him. When Jesus asks them why, they say they will stone him for blasphemy because, "You, a mere man, claim to be God."

Jesus responds by pointing to the infallibility of Scripture:

> It is written in your own Scriptures that God said to certain leaders of the people, "I say, you are gods!" And you know that the Scriptures cannot be altered. So if those people who received God's message were called "gods," why do you call it blasphemy when I say, "I am the Son of God"? After all, the Father set me apart and sent me into the world.
>
> JOHN 10:34-36

Jesus stated plainly, "The Scriptures cannot be altered." The New King James translation reads, "The Scripture cannot be broken." A broken word is an untrue word. Nothing can break God's Word. We can throw our questions at Scripture, but we can't break it. God's Word is eternal, and therefore unbreakable. It is perfect, and therefore incorruptible. It is complete, and therefore indestructible. God's Word cannot be altered.

Three Reasons You Can Trust the Entire Bible

"The Word of God" refers to two things. First, "the Word" is a name given to Jesus:

> In the beginning the Word already existed.
>   The Word was with God,
>   and the Word was God.
>
> JOHN 1:1

> He wore a robe dipped in blood, and his title was the Word of God.
>
> REVELATION 19:13

Second, "the Word" is Scripture, God's message to humanity in written form. The Word of God (the Bible) points us to the Word who *is* God (Jesus Christ).

Just as Christ the Word came and dwelt among us in physical form, so too we have the written Word of God to help us live as Christ lived. And there's an interesting parallel here. Just as Jesus is fully human and fully God, so too is the Bible fully human (written by human hands) and fully divine (inspired by God).

What does that mean?

It means that, though the pages of Scripture were inked by human hands, the Bible is nevertheless fully God's Word. The Bible is not simply a collection of words *about* God; it is divinely inspired words *from* God. Though these words were written at specific times and places, they are nevertheless eternal. The Bible transcends time and place to speak to all humanity in every generation and culture. That's why the writer of Hebrews could say, "The word of God is alive and powerful" (Hebrews 4:12).

Just as Jesus is eternally alive, so too the Bible is eternally alive

(Psalm 119:89; Isaiah 40:8). Grasping the power of the written Word is one thing, but believing the written Word is *alive* is entirely different. The Bible is God's own words, given to us for the purpose of drawing people to himself.

Because the Bible is from God, it is personal communication from him. We can trust that the Bible is true because it is authoritative, inspired, infallible, and sufficient.

1. The Bible Is Authoritative

Understanding the Bible as a whole requires us to submit to the authority of God's Word. Often, our problem is that we want to know God on our own terms, not his. But we can't get into someone's heart any way we want. We can't love someone exclusively on our own terms. The same dynamic exists with God and his Word.

The Bible is full of God's love, but you cannot approach this love any way you want. You are not the authority over the Bible. Rather, the Bible is the authority over you. Do not read the Bible like you're going through junk-mail envelopes, looking for a deal and then tossing the rest aside without even opening it. Do not read the Bible like you might read the opinion section of the newspaper, looking for an angle that supports a viewpoint you already have. Instead, read the Bible like a love letter. Devour every word and feel each phrase. The Bible is the most profound message of love ever written. Indeed, the Bible's words define love. So don't just search the Scriptures. Let the Scriptures search you.

2. The Bible Is Inspired and Infallible

When you read the Bible, you are hearing directly from God. The Bible is inspired by God, which means it is "God-breathed" (2 Timothy 3:16, NIV). As such, the Bible is infallible; it will not lead you astray. You can trust the Bible.

To say the Bible is *inspired* by God means that the Holy Spirit prompted and guided the authors. Every word was God's intention. Luke records many details in his Gospel, but those details were revealed by God. Paul's letter to the Philippians conveys the joy Paul had for the church, but God gave Paul the words to express his joy. The Psalms give voice to the highs and lows of David's emotions, but God directed the words of poetry.

To say the Bible is *infallible* means it is incapable of error. When Jesus prayed for his disciples, he said, "Make them holy by your truth; teach them your word, which is truth" (John 17:17). All truth is derived from God, which means the Bible is the gold standard of truth. It will not deceive us or prove unreliable. Speaking through the prophet Isaiah, God says of his Word, "I send it out, and it always produces fruit. It will accomplish all I want it to, and it will prosper everywhere I send it" (Isaiah 55:11). Because God's Word is infallible, it is wholly reliable—always and everywhere.

3. The Bible Is Sufficient

God's Word is all you need for living in a way that honors him. Nothing else is needed to understand the Good News of Jesus. No other books are required to know God and follow the Holy Spirit. When David wrote Psalm 19, he recorded several aspects of the Bible's sufficiency.

> The instructions of the LORD are perfect,
>   reviving the soul.
> The decrees of the LORD are trustworthy,
>   making wise the simple.
> The commandments of the LORD are right,
>   bringing joy to the heart.

The commands of the LORD are clear,
   giving insight for living.
Reverence for the LORD is pure,
   lasting forever.
The laws of the LORD are true;
   each one is fair.
They are more desirable than gold,
   even the finest gold.
They are sweeter than honey,
   even honey dripping from the comb.
They are a warning to your servant,
   a great reward for those who obey them.

PSALM 19:7-11

What we have in the Bible is perfect, trustworthy, right, clear, pure, and true. No other written word can make such a claim. The Bible alone is all-sufficient.

An Invitation to Read the Bestselling Book of All Time

Not only is the Bible the bestselling book of all time, but I've heard it is also the most shoplifted book. For more than two thousand years, debates have raged over the Bible. Leaders have taken oaths with a hand placed on the Bible. Governments have banned the Bible. Many people seem to have an opinion about the Bible, even if they've never read it. The Bible is as popular as it is notorious. Yes, the Bible is the bestselling book of all time, but it is so much more.[3]

If you don't have your Bible near you, take a minute to go get it. Prayerfully ask God to give you a passion for reading his Word. In the next chapter, you'll learn more about how to read your

Bible. But don't wait. Open your Bible now and read it, even if only for a few minutes. Then come back and we'll continue our discussion.

1

Understanding
the Beginning

The Origins of the Bible

THE BIBLE YOU READ was printed or downloaded at a specific point in time. Ink went to paper and pages were bound together, or computer programming sent data from a server to your device. Maybe your Bible is on your phone. Maybe you have a sentimental family heirloom Bible you read. Or perhaps you've started using new technology such as the Filament Bible to dive deep into God's Word. There is nothing sacred about the form your Bible takes, whether printed or digital. What makes the Bible sacred is the origin of the words it contains. They come from God.

How the Bible Came to Be

The Bible consists of sixty-six books—thirty-nine in the Old Testament and twenty-seven in the New Testament. It is not a list of propositions or orders from on high, dictated to a reluctantly subservient people. Though every word is inspired by the Holy Spirit, the words themselves were written by human beings—people with their own personalities and life experiences, writing in their own time and context. In this chapter, we will explore how all these writings came together to form what we now know as the Bible.

Who Wrote the Books of the Bible?

Ultimately, it is God who determines his own Word. But from a human perspective, there was a way in which God revealed Scripture to humanity. Approximately forty authors wrote the books of the Bible over the course of about 1,600 years. The authorship of some of the books is unattributed or the subject of debate. Some authors chose not to include their name on the books they wrote. For example, we are unsure who wrote Esther in the Old Testament and Hebrews in the New Testament. Other books, like the Psalms, have multiple contributors.

The writers of the Bible came from various backgrounds. Moses was an adopted prince who became a shepherd. David was a shepherd who became a king. Matthew was a tax collector. Peter and John were fishermen. And Luke was a physician.

Even though the Bible was written by a diverse group of authors spanning multiple centuries, it is a coherent and cohesive whole. Scripture does not contradict itself, nor does it contain errors. The authors of the Bible write from many perspectives, but all converge in one place. Consistently, the Bible tells God's story of redeeming the people he loves through the salvation of Jesus Christ.

Where Did the First Manuscripts Originate?

In the ancient world, writing was a specialized skill. Everything was done by hand. Few people owned anything written. The Old

Testament was written mainly in Hebrew and some Aramaic (parts of Daniel and Ezra). The earliest copies of the books of the Hebrew Bible would have existed on papyrus or vellum. Papyrus was made of plant fibers. Vellum was made of animal skins.

During the time of Alexander the Great, Greek became one of the world's most widely spoken languages. It was during this time that Jewish scholars in Egypt began to translate the Hebrew Old Testament into Greek. Seventy scribes worked on the translation and produced what is known as the Septuagint (meaning *seventy*). The writers of the New Testament wrote in Greek and would have been familiar with the Septuagint.

Until the printing press was invented around 1440, the books of the Bible were copied by hand. Thousands of these hand-written texts still exist, including the Codex Vaticanus and Codex Sinaiticus, two ancient Greek manuscripts containing most of the Old and New Testaments.

In 1947, a Bedouin shepherd looking for a lost goat made a fascinating discovery. In the caves of Qumran, he found scrolls and papyrus fragments containing portions of the Old Testament and other Hebrew and Greek manuscripts dating to the Alexandrian era. These documents and others demonstrated the careful precision with which the scribes had copied the texts.

As Christianity spread from Jerusalem to Judea to Samaria and to the ends of the earth, the New Testament was translated into Ethiopic, Coptic, Slavonic, Armenian, Syriac, and many other languages.[1] In the fourth century, Pope Damasus commissioned what became the Vulgate, a Latin version of the Hebrew Old Testament and Greek New Testament.

One of the oldest fragments of the Hebrew Bible dates to the seventh century BC, during the time of Jeremiah the prophet. This fragment contains the priestly blessing from Numbers 6. The oldest fragments of the New Testament are from John's Gospel and date to about AD 125.

Did God's message get lost among the variety of authors and translators over the course of time? It's a reasonable question. But with the Bible handed down through history and all the various manuscripts discovered over the past few centuries, the accuracy from one to the next is nothing short of miraculous. In one example, comparing a portion of Isaiah found on a Qumran scroll with the Codex Leningradensis, the text is virtually identical, even though a thousand years separate these two manuscripts.[2] You can be confident that the Bible you have today is an accurate representation of God's Word.

Who Decided Which Books to Include in the Old and New Testaments?

The word *canon* is often used to describe the books of the Bible considered authoritative by Christians. As previously mentioned, the Christian canon includes sixty-six books—thirty-nine books in the Old Testament and twenty-seven books in the New Testament.

By the time of Christ, the Jewish community had generally agreed upon the Hebrew canon, which Christians refer to as the Old Testament. For the most part, the New Testament canon took shape by the second century and was considered officially settled by the fourth century. The canonicity of New Testament books was largely determined by their connection to one of the apostles, consistent doctrine, and their overall acceptance by the early church.[3]

How Did We Get the English Language Versions of the Bible We Read Today?

Though portions of the Bible had been translated from Latin to Old English as early as the seventh century, it was English theologian and priest John Wycliffe who first translated the entire Bible into Middle English in the 1300s. At the time, the Bible used in worship services was written in Latin, which meant that only the privileged classes and religious hierarchy, who had access to the necessary education and training, were able to read and understand Scripture. As a result, the common people were not able to access and learn from Scripture directly. Wycliffe believed every person had the right to read and interpret the Bible, and he began work with his colleague Nicholas of Hereford to translate the Latin Bible into English. Their versions were later revised by John Purvey. After completion of the project, and following his death, Wycliffe was labeled a heretic because his ideas and criticism of corruption threatened the power structure of the religious system at the time.

The next significant figure in the development of the English Bible was William Tyndale, who used a printing press to publish his version of the Bible. Where Wycliffe had translated the Bible from Latin, Tyndale used copies of the original Hebrew and Greek texts.

Tyndale's dedication to distributing God's Word came with consequences, however. Both the English monarchy and the religious authorities were threatened by the idea of people reading the Bible for themselves. In 1536, ten years after publishing his Bible, Tyndale was strangled to death at the stake and his body burned.

Before the execution, Tyndale spoke his final words: "Lord, open the eyes of the king of England!"[4] He gave his life to open the eyes of people through the reading of God's Word. Wycliffe and Tyndale had begun an ongoing movement of translating the Bible into common languages. They knew the power of reading Scripture and wanted everyone to experience this joy. Today, translators are working to bring the Bible to many more languages, even lesser known and obscure ones.

In 1560, William Whittingham produced the Geneva Bible, which was used by John Bunyan and the Puritans and was the first version of the Bible to use verse numbers. In 1611, King James authorized the version of the Bible that bears his name to this day, and it became the most widely read version of the Bible in history. About 250 years later, the church recognized the need to modernize the language of the King James Version, and the English Revised Version went to press in 1885. The American Standard Version followed in 1901.

Today, many modern translations of the Bible are available, including the New International Version, the New Living Translation, and the English Standard Version, among many others. Amazingly, the Bible has now been translated into more than seven hundred languages!

Which English Language Version of the Bible Is Best?

The fact that there are differences among the various translations is attributable in part to the translation philosophy or approach used by each group of translators. Scholars use two primary approaches when translating the Bible: *formal equivalence* and *dynamic equivalence.*

Formal equivalence prioritizes the best word-for-word translation of the original languages. As a result, these translations sometimes have stiff or awkward phrasing when the Hebrew and Greek texts don't translate directly into English. The New American Standard Bible and the King James Version are examples of formal equivalence translations.

In contrast to the word-for-word approach of formal equivalence, dynamic equivalence (or functional equivalence) uses a thought-for-thought approach and prioritizes the readability of the text. The New International Version and the New Living Translation are examples of dynamic equivalence.

Which translation approach is the best? In most cases, both translation philosophies produce highly accurate translations of the text. But it's important to note that neither approach provides a purely literal translation. Why not? In some cases, literal translation is impossible because there is no English equivalent for a Hebrew or Greek word or phrase. Or there may be multiple words in the original language and only one equivalent word in English. For example, while English has just one word for *love*, Greek has four (*agape, eros, philia,* and *storge.*) Hebrew and Greek also make use of euphemisms for sex and matters of the toilet that would make no sense if translated literally. Systems of weights and measures, and other culturally bound artifacts have changed since the time of the Bible, and some ideas and words are notoriously difficult to translate. The better English translations typically include margin notes to explain difficult texts.

When reading your Bible, it is a good practice to use one main translation. Having a go-to version helps with retention and Scripture memory. For example, I prefer to use the New Living Translation (NLT) for most of my personal reading and preaching. The NLT is both highly accurate and easy to read. I also use the New American Standard Bible (NASB) for theological study. Because most of the Scripture I memorized as a child is from the New King James Version (NKJV), I tend to quote the NKJV when relying on memory. When I want to read the Bible poetically, I might dig into the King James Version, which is famous and valued for its use of colorful Early Modern English. In short, different translations can be used in different ways. Pick one that suits your purpose, and you may be more inclined to enjoy reading Scripture.

TOP TEN BIBLE TRANSLATIONS

According to the Evangelical Christian Publishing Association (ECPA), these are the top ten bestselling Bible translations in the US:[5]

1. New International Version (dynamic)
2. King James Version (formal)
3. New Living Translation (dynamic)
4. English Standard Version (formal)
5. New King James Version (formal)
6. Christian Standard Bible (formal)
7. Reina Valera (formal Spanish)
8. New International Reader's Version (dynamic)
9. *The Message* (dynamic)[6]
10. New American Standard Bible (formal)

Bible translators are committed to accurately representing the wording of the original Hebrew, Aramaic, and Greek texts. One major issue in translating the Bible from the original languages is that the original autographs written by the original authors no longer exist. But this should not cause despair. Frankly, I believe God sovereignly intended for us not to have the originals. The temptation would be too great to worship them as icons instead of using them to point us to Jesus. Nevertheless, we have thousands of copies, some dating close to the time of the originals, which means that translators can sift through the ancient texts to check for variants and remove potential errors.

Through the process of textual criticism, translators weigh the internal evidence of manuscripts (e.g., how many and what kind of mistakes did a specific scribe make?) and external evidence of manuscripts (e.g., what is the quality and age of the document?) to arrive at the best available translation. New manuscript discoveries help refine this process and give us a high level of confidence that our modern English Bibles accurately convey what God wants us to know.

Connecting the Two Testaments

Central to both the Old Testament and the New Testament is the concept of *covenant*. In fact, *testament* means *covenant* in the original languages of the Bible. Thus the Old and New Testaments are sometimes referred to as the Old and New Covenants.

The division between old and new doesn't mean that one replaced the other or that one is more important than the other. Rather, the Old Testament and the New Testament both reveal God's story of redeeming us, first through a promise and then through the fulfillment of that promise.

The Old Testament reveals a *promise* from God. That promise is referred to as the old covenant.[7] A covenant is an agreement or contract between two parties. After the fall into sin of Adam and Eve, which broke the relationship between God and humanity, God made a series of covenants to reconcile with his people. Though God's people repeatedly failed to uphold their part of the covenants, God remained faithful. The Old Testament depicts God as intensely seeking a relationship with humanity, motivated by unconditional love.

The New Testament reveals the *fulfillment* of God's promise. Where the old covenant contains a promise of redemption, the new covenant contains the fulfillment of that promise of redemption in Christ Jesus. Through the death and resurrection of Jesus, God offers salvation to those who repent of their sins and believe in Jesus. The promise of salvation revealed in the Old Testament is fulfilled in Christ and made eternally secure by the Holy Spirit. Both the Old and the New Testaments affirm Jesus as the only way to salvation.

God's story in the Bible is continuous. While the Bible is arranged in two testaments written by more than forty human authors, the thread woven throughout the entire story is God's plan of redemption for humanity. The Old Testament is about the covenant of God's law. The New Testament is about the covenant of God's grace. What begins with God and his chosen people in Genesis, ends with Christ and the church in Revelation.

Three Key Principles for Understanding God's Word

Many people know the power of God's Word but are perplexed once they begin reading it. It's hard to admit we don't get it! Some of this confusion stems from spiritual warfare and a lack of discipline to obey God. But many will try to read God's Word only to stop because they think they don't understand. The next few sections will help you recognize what you are reading.

1. Interpretation: Understanding the Plain Meaning

As you read the Bible, one key to understanding is to ask the question, "What is the plain meaning of the text?" Most passages of Scripture have a clear story line with identifiable characters and themes. Though this question may seem simple enough, the best theologians throughout church history have often differed on the "plain meaning" of various Bible passages. This includes verses about such issues as mode of baptism, roles of men and women in the church, and whether or not one can lose one's salvation. What seems plain to me may not seem plain to you! In fact, as a pastor, I've made it clear to my congregation that I do not expect them to come to the same conclusions I do with every text. Well-meaning people can read parts of Scripture and come to different conclusions. A rule of thumb for navigating such differences is the maxim, "In essentials, unity. In nonessentials, liberty. In all things, love."

When your interpretation leads you to a completely novel view of Scripture, one that contradicts other biblical teaching or traditionally held views, be cautious. Countless theologians across two thousand years of church history have worked to interpret the Bible. Though there are differing views of Scripture, these views are well-documented and common. Views that contradict traditional interpretations are in danger of being heretical. A view of Scripture becomes heretical when it departs from accepted or orthodox beliefs and warps the meaning of the gospel. Some of the sternest warnings in Scripture are reserved for those who abuse God's Word by shifting away from the gospel message of Jesus.

As you read God's Word, ask the simple question, "What is the plain meaning of the text?" If you are still stumped, a good next step is to consult a respected reference book such as a study Bible, a commentary, a Bible encyclopedia, or a Bible dictionary.

2. Genres and Exegesis: Understanding the Original Intent

When reading Scripture, it's important to understand the authors' original intent. This requires understanding what genre of literature each book of the Bible belongs to, and also how to exegete or analyze it to discern the text's original context and meaning.

A literary *genre* is a kind or category of writing. One of the things that makes the Bible fun to read is that it contains many different genres, including law, poetry, history, letters, prophecy, wisdom literature, and apocalyptic literature. Each genre has a unique purpose that provides a context for understanding its original intent, which is why we read legal documents differently than we read poetry or a personal letter.

When we don't know the genre of biblical literature, it's easier to get lost. For example, those who try to read through the Bible from beginning to end often joke about giving up in despair when they hit the book of Leviticus. Why? Because it's a collection of civil, ceremonial, and moral laws, which isn't exactly scintillating reading. But when we know up front that we are reading a collection of legal writings, then we're better prepared for the content. The Psalms are another example of how it helps to understand genre. Some of David's psalms include disturbing expressions of anger and violence, which can make them difficult to read. However, when we understand he is wrestling with raw emotions through poetry, rather than acting in anger and violence, it's easier to connect to the evocative nature of his poems.

Exegesis is the process of analyzing a text to understand not only the literary context but also the historical context. Every part of the Bible was written in a specific place and time. David agonizes about his sin in some of the psalms. Habakkuk cries out to God because of injustice. Paul writes with joy to the Philippian church. The imagery in the book of Revelation is viewed through John's first-century eyes as he tries to explain God's vision to him. God sovereignly wanted us to receive this revelation through John's perspective, but it is helpful to know his descriptions are based upon his perspective. When we exegete Scripture, we are attempting to draw the original meaning *out of* the text. We should never read our opinions *into* the text. The historical and literary contexts are crucial to getting exegesis correct. When someone takes a single verse out of context to prove a point, that person is reading his or her opinions into the text rather than drawing the original meaning out of the text.

3. Hermeneutics: Understanding the Application

Broadly speaking, hermeneutics, as a field of study within theology, involves the entire process of understanding Scripture. More specifically, hermeneutics is about uncovering the contemporary relevance of specific text. Hermeneutics asks the question, "What does this text mean for me right now?" Interpretation and exegesis help you understand Scripture in its past context. Hermeneutics helps you apply Scripture in the present.

The Bible contains some of the world's greatest stories, teaching, and wisdom. To absorb the truth of the Bible, you must reflect on it devotionally and apply it personally. Frankly, the Bible should change your life! While there is value in retaining the information in the Bible, the greater purpose of Scripture is to transform you from the inside out and to help you live a different kind of life. If the Bible does not change the way you live, then you're not reading it correctly.

Bible scholar George Guthrie refers to meditation as "mentally chewing" on a part of God's Word.[8] As you read, notice the words, phrases, or sentences that catch your attention. Reread those passages several times. Reflect prayerfully on those words and phrases, asking God for insights on how you are to live out the verse or passage you are reading. Make notes in a journal. The process of writing by hand helps imprint the content on your mind and in your heart. Prayerful and consistent devotion to God's Word helps fill your tank to give you the gas to live. Reading God's Word for information or out of duty can quickly become drudgery, but reading God's Word for personal growth and change leads to delight.

Where Are You in Scripture?

Though the Bible is first of all a story about God, the Bible is also a story of God's holy and gracious effort to reconcile with his people—with you and me. Our names may not be written on the pages of the Bible, but we are nevertheless part of God's epic story.

When you read Scripture, don't view God as the missing piece of your life. You will find no satisfaction in believing that a little bit of God will fill in the gaps. You don't need God to complete *your* story. Rather, you are part of *God's* story. As the history of the world unfolds, every person fits into God's sovereign plan. When you realize that God is not the missing piece for *you*, but that *you* are a piece to *his* master work, you will begin to grasp the true meaning of Scripture. You will find God when you *immerse* yourself in his Word.

PART I

THE OLD TESTAMENT

2

God's Law

The Five Scrolls and Instructions for Life

THE FIRST FIVE BOOKS in the Old Testament—Genesis, Exodus, Leviticus, Numbers, and Deuteronomy—are often referred to as the Pentateuch. The term is a combination of the Greek words *penta* (five) and *teuchos* (scroll or writing implement). These five books tell God's story from the Creation account up to the point at which the Israelites are about to conquer the Promised Land.

The five books of the Pentateuch contain more than six hundred laws. They include civil rules, ceremonial procedures, and moral absolutes. Their purpose was to direct attention and worship to God. The Israelites were expected to keep these laws as a sign of their devotion to him.

In the Jewish tradition, these same five books are referred to as the Torah, usually translated "law," but the term has a deeper meaning. *Torah* conveys the idea not just of rules but also of teaching and instruction. The five books of the law thus contain instructions for life. God's law is not a burdensome list of prohibitions; rather, it tells us how to live a life that is pleasing to God.

Four major themes emerge in these books: God's sovereignty (complete control), theological history, salvation, and holiness. God creates everything in Genesis out of nothing (*creatio ex nihilo*). The foundational elements of Israel's history emerge in the law. The theological foundations of the Bible are rooted in historical events, not in folklore or myths. In these books we learn about the fallen condition of humanity and how everyone needs salvation. God did not save his people grudgingly, out of a sense of obligation. He actively pursued them with a heart of grace and mercy. The standard of holiness is set. The law shows us how we are to be holy as God is holy.

Genesis is the story of Creation and a book of beginnings. Exodus is a compelling story of salvation and redemption. Leviticus reveals that a life of holiness is the only way to please God and the only reasonable response to his grace. In Numbers, the people wander from God in sin and disobedience. The Pentateuch concludes with Deuteronomy, a book of renewal and affirmation of God's goodness.

When the Israelites, the Hebrew people, followed God's law, he blessed them. When they disobeyed God's law, he offered numerous warnings and ultimately judged them if they did not return to the practice of obedience.

A pattern emerges in the books of the law and carries into the rest of the Old Testament. People sin. God offers mercy. The people accept his mercy but sin again. God warns of judgment if they continue to sin. The people ignore God. Judgment comes, and people cry out to God for mercy. God offers mercy. And the cycle begins all over again. Book after book, this pattern develops.

And that's the point. The Old Testament, specifically the law, exists to reveal the need for a Savior.

Genesis: God Creates

The first book of the Bible provides essential background and foundation for understanding the events leading up to the formation of the nation of Israel.[1] It begins with a sweeping account of Creation. The truths of the Bible are built on the events recorded in Genesis, but there is much more to come.

Understanding Genesis is an exercise in wanting to know more. The world begins, but we are left wondering how it will end. Humanity sins, but the full consequences of those actions are not yet realized. The promise of salvation is introduced, but we do not fully grasp how God will save his people. The book opens with God creating life and concludes with the death of Joseph. Both life and death begin in Genesis. The rest of the Bible examines the great conflict between the life God wants for his people and the death they choose instead.

Genesis 3 details the cataclysmic fall of humanity. Adam and Eve sinned in the Garden of Eden because they fell into Satan's trap of deceit. All three must face the consequences of sin. God tells Adam and Eve that the joys of both work and birthing children will now come through painful labor. But God first addresses the deceiving serpent, Satan.

In the Bible's first reference to the coming Savior, God tells Satan, "He will strike your head, and you will strike his heel" (Genesis 3:15). From the beginning, we learn that Satan is defeated. The great deceiver may be able to wound Jesus on the cross (the striking of his heel), but Jesus will give the fatal blow to Satan (the striking of his head) by defeating death, evil, sin, and injustice.

Four major events and four major characters provide the structure for the fifty chapters in this book of beginnings. The events occur in Genesis 1–11, and the characters are highlighted in Genesis 12–50.

Four Major Events

The Creation Account with Adam and Eve (Genesis 1–2)

The Fall of Humanity into Sin (Genesis 3–5)

The Flooding of Earth and Noah's Ark (Genesis 6–9)

The Crisis of the Tower of Babel (Genesis 10–11)

Four Major Characters

Abraham and a Covenant of Faith (Genesis 12–25)

Isaac and a Chosen Lineage (Genesis 24–28)

Jacob and the Formation of Israel (Genesis 27–36)

Joseph and the Rescue of Israel (Genesis 37–50)

Even as God selects these events and places these characters within the biblical story, it is God himself who is the true hero of Genesis, a theme that continues throughout the rest of the Bible. Though God works through events and people, his sovereign purpose rises above the actions and events of human history.

Exodus: God Saves

While the book of Genesis traces a family history through Abraham, Isaac, Jacob, and Joseph, the book of Exodus covers the start of the national history of Israel. About 350 years have passed between the events at the end of Genesis and those at the beginning of Exodus. As Genesis concludes, seventy members of Jacob's family have traveled from Canaan to Egypt to escape famine. At the start of Exodus, Jacob's descendants have increased to the point that they outnumber the Egyptians. Perceiving the potential threat this poses to his power, a new Egyptian pharaoh has enslaved and mistreated the Israelites. But God has not forgotten the promise he made to Abraham (who was called Abram at the time): "I will make you into a great nation" (Genesis 12:2). Exodus is the record of how God rescued his people from slavery and delivered them to Mount Sinai to receive his law and to build the Tabernacle, the portable tent in which God promised to meet with his people (Exodus 29:42).

Exodus has two main themes about salvation. First, God rescues the people through a chosen deliverer, Moses. Second, God pursues a relationship with the people through the law and the Tabernacle. The structure of Exodus demonstrates these two major themes.

The Flight from Egypt (Exodus 1–18)
    God's power is revealed in deliverance.
    The Hebrew people are brought out of slavery and
        given freedom.

The Law Is Given (Exodus 19–24)
    God's holiness is revealed in salvation.
    The Hebrew people are brought under the law and
        given a responsibility.

The Tabernacle Is Built (Exodus 25–40)
    God's wisdom is revealed in worship.
    The Hebrew people are brought into fellowship
        with God.

Moses is the central character in the Exodus story. At the time when Moses is born in Egypt, Pharaoh has ordered the killing of all male Hebrew infants to reduce the threat posed by the large number of Israelites then in slavery. To save Moses' life, his family sets him in the Nile River in a basket, only for him to be discovered and rescued by Pharaoh's daughter. When she decides to raise Moses as her own, he becomes royalty and enjoys all the benefits and privileges of palace life. However, his circumstances take a sudden and dramatic turn when, at the age of forty, he kills an Egyptian while trying to protect a Hebrew man from abuse. He then flees to the desert and spends the next forty years as a shepherd.

Moses is eighty when God calls him to return to Egypt to deliver the Israelites from slavery. He is a reluctant leader. Though God is determined to save the Israelites, Moses is determined to forget his past in Egypt. Through a series of events, God redeems Moses and reconnects him to his family. God uses Moses, together with his brother, Aaron, to send a series of plagues on the Egyptians that ultimately force Pharaoh into releasing the Israelites. Exodus is about the deliverance of God's people and their long journey toward the Promised Land.

As the Israelites travel through the wilderness, God gives them a summary of his law in the Ten Commandments (Exodus 20:1-17). The first four commandments are about how God's people are to relate to God. The next six commandments are about how God's people are to relate to one another. These ten laws are a summary of the entirety of God's law: *We need to be right with God, and we need to be right with others.*

In the New Testament, when the Pharisees ask Jesus to name the greatest commandment, he answers, "'You must love the LORD your God with all your heart, all your soul, and all your mind.' This is the first and greatest commandment. A second is equally important: 'Love your neighbor as yourself'" (Matthew 22:37-39). In summarizing the Ten Commandments, he summarizes the entire law. He recognizes that *all* of the law is important.

Exodus concludes with a long description of the Tabernacle, covering several chapters. In fact, Scripture devotes more words to the description of the Tabernacle than it does to any other single object in the Bible. Why? In the Old Testament, the Tabernacle was God's way of demonstrating his presence among his people. As the place where sacrifices were offered, the Tabernacle also pointed to Jesus. In the New Testament, we learn that Jesus "made his home among us," or literally "tabernacled" with us (John 1:14). The Tabernacle was central to Jewish identity and religious life. It was where the Jewish priests interceded for the people and offered sacrifices, and it was where God revealed himself and his will.

All the functions signified by the Tabernacle as a meeting place for God and human beings have now been fully realized in Jesus, who fulfilled the sacrificial requirements of the law. The deliverance of God's people from slavery, the giving of the Ten Commandments, and the creation of the Tabernacle all point to the redemption ultimately found in Christ. Exodus is a beautiful foretelling of salvation in Jesus!

Leviticus: God Is Holy

In Genesis, humanity falls into sin. In Exodus, God redeems humanity. In Leviticus, God provides rules and guidelines governing the proper way to worship him. The events of Leviticus take place about a year after the Israelites have been redeemed from slavery. As they are camped at the base of Mount Sinai in the wilderness, the Hebrew people learn about God's holiness and how they are expected to worship. Throughout the book, God reminds the people, "I am holy."

Leviticus is named for the Levites, descendants of Levi, one of Jacob's (Israel's) twelve sons. Moses and Aaron were of the tribe of Levi, and God chose Aaron and his family to serve the people as priests. Leviticus is, in a sense, an instruction manual for the priesthood. Exodus explains the proper *place* of worship—the Tabernacle. Leviticus explains the proper *mode* of worship—the sacrifices and feasts. The people "get right with God" through the sacrifices, and they "stay right" through the celebration of designated feasts.[2]

Three general categories of law—moral, civil, and ceremonial—emerge in Leviticus. Moral laws concern issues of justice and judgment. The Ten Commandments are an example of moral laws. Civil laws regulate the way people interact with each other. An example of a civil law is how to make restitution when someone is gored by an ox (Exodus 21:28-36). Ceremonial laws apply to rituals and sacrifices within the Hebrew community, such as the grooming requirements for priests (Leviticus 21:5). The moral laws transcend their original context and apply broadly to all societies in all times, even in our culture today. Most of the civil and ceremonial laws were specific to the ancient Hebrew community and were ultimately fulfilled in Christ. Even though we do not follow many of the regulations in Leviticus today, they are still valuable in that they point us to Christ in the New Testament.

Initially, the placement of Leviticus within the Pentateuch might seem odd. Why interrupt the story of the Exodus with a bunch of detailed rules for living and instructions for worship? It breaks the narrative flow of the rest of the Pentateuch. The events portrayed at the end of Exodus do not pick up again until Numbers 11. But don't be fooled by the placement. It is intentional. Leviticus is a call to holiness and an integral part of what God wants from the Israelites as they anticipate entering the

Promised Land. Included in this call to holiness are the sacrificial system and the installation of Israel's priests.

> The Five Major Types of Sacrifices (Exodus 1–7)
> > Burnt offering: presented to make atonement for sin
> > Grain offering: given to express thankfulness
> > Peace offering: done during the feast days for restoration
> > Sin offering: purging of impurities and cleansing for offenses against God
> > Guilt offering: used for restitution to God
>
> Ordination and Installation of the Priesthood (Exodus 8–10)
>
> Laws of What Is Clean and Unclean in Everyday Life (Exodus 11–16)
>
> The Holiness Code and Acceptance with God (Exodus 17–27)

Leviticus provides detailed guidelines or holiness codes for how God's people can live in right relationship with him and with each other. These codes of holiness apply to conduct both within and beyond the Tabernacle. God is perfectly holy. It is his nature. As humans, we are not intrinsically holy. Throughout Leviticus, God introduces the concept of atonement, how an unholy people can be reconciled to a holy God. The ritual sacrifices in Leviticus point to the ultimate sacrifice that Jesus would make "once for all time" when he fulfilled the requirements of the sacrificial system (1 Peter 3:18).

Numbers: God's People Wander

Two words summarize the book of Numbers: *murmurings* and *wanderings*. For forty years, the Israelites meander through the wilderness and complain. God takes his people from Mount Sinai through Kadesh and to the border of Canaan on the plains of Moab, the Promised Land. A trip that should take a few weeks ends up lasting decades. God wants to prepare the Hebrews for a military conquest of the land he has promised them, but his people fail to remain faithful. As a consequence, they wander in the desert.

Numbers gets its title because it contains two censuses of the Israelites—one near the beginning of their desert wanderings and the other near the end (Numbers 1; 26). Along with the censuses, Numbers also includes laws, narratives, and a genealogy of Aaron's family. The flow of the text wanders almost as much as God's people wander in the wilderness. Though the book is less clearly organized than the rest of the Pentateuch, the overall structure is evident in two ways: the two generations and their geographic movements.

Generations	Geographic Movements
Old Generation (Numbers 1–14)	At Mount Sinai (Numbers 1:10–10:10)
Wanderings (Numbers 15–20)	Mount Sinai to Edom (Numbers 10:11–20:21)
New Generation (Numbers 21–36)	Edom to the Jordan River (Numbers 20:22–36:13)

Five key characters are present in Numbers: Moses, Aaron, Miriam, Joshua, and Caleb. Moses is Israel's leader. Aaron, Moses' brother, is Israel's high priest. Miriam is a prophet and the sister of Moses and Aaron. In Numbers 12, she is struck with leprosy for criticizing Moses, God's chosen leader for Israel. Joshua and Caleb are heroes who believe God's promise and become the only two people in their generation to enter the Promised Land.

What do the Israelites learn as they wander? They learn to trust God to supply their needs. When they lack organization, God gives them leaders (Numbers 1). When they are hungry, God gives them food (Numbers 11). When they are thirsty, God gives them water (Numbers 20). When they need direction and reassurance, God gives them guidance and his presence through a pillar of cloud by day and a pillar of fire by night (Numbers 9; 14).

The story of Balaam and his donkey (Numbers 22–24) is one of the most fascinating in all the Pentateuch, as God uses a Mesopotamian prophet to announce his intentions for the Hebrew people. The story teaches us that God fulfills his covenant even when his people are passively wandering without direction.

At the core of Israel's wandering is a worship problem. They need to learn to worship on God's terms, not their own. Whereas Exodus shows the people *where* to worship (the Tabernacle), and Leviticus shows *how* they should worship (through the sacrifices), Numbers gives an account of how God's people *wander* from worship. Israel fails in worship because of sexual immorality, rejection of authority, and a complaining spirit. Ultimately even Moses and Aaron are not allowed to enter the Promised Land because they fail to obey God completely. Numbers concludes with a new generation preparing to enter the Promised Land. All is not lost. God remains faithful.

Deuteronomy: God's People Are Renewed

The finish line is in sight. After decades of wilderness walking, the Israelites are ready to enter the land God had promised them after he delivered them from slavery in Egypt. The events in the book take place in one location—on the side of the Jordan River across from the city of Jericho. While the events in Numbers take place over forty years, the events in Deuteronomy cover about sixty days, thirty of which are devoted to mourning for Moses upon his death.

The name of the book derives from two Greek words: *deuteros* (meaning "second") and *nomos* (meaning "law"). Deuteronomy represents a second giving of the original law—not a new law. The same covenant is given in a new setting to a new generation as Moses expounds upon the law's meaning for a generation who grew up in the wilderness and have no firsthand knowledge of slavery in Egypt.

Deuteronomy has several purposes. As one generation transitions to the next, Moses transitions leadership to Joshua. The people prepare to transition from wandering to settling in a new land, where they will receive a new revelation of God's love. Additionally, this final book of Moses contains more about God's love than the rest of the Pentateuch. God's love is revealed as the thread that ties together the purpose of his law. Deuteronomy is also a literary bridge between the five books of law and the historical books that follow. Moses looks *backward* as he summarizes the themes of the Pentateuch and finalizes the law. Moses looks *forward* as he prepares the Israelites for their future in the Promised Land.

The structure of Deuteronomy is organized around three addresses of Moses, with an appendix at the end.

First Address: Moses Looks Back on the Law Given
(Deuteronomy 1:1–4:43)

Second Address: Moses Looks Up to God Alone
(Deuteronomy 4:44–26:19)

Third Address: Moses Looks Forward to What Is Coming
(Deuteronomy 27:1–31:29)

Appendix: The Song, Blessing, and Death of Moses
(Deuteronomy 31:30–34:12)

The first address recounts God's work on Israel's behalf. Moses retells the story of the people, beginning with the Exodus, and urges them to obey God's commands. He concludes by giving them a stern warning against idolatry and reminding them of their calling to serve the one true God.

The second address restates the covenant laws originally presented in Exodus 20–23. Moses reviews the Ten Commandments and gives instructions on how to teach the commandments to succeeding generations. The second address also contains a significant expression called the *shema*: "Listen, O Israel! The LORD is our God, the LORD alone" (Deuteronomy 6:4). The *shema* (pronounced shə-MAH) is both a declaration of faith and a prayer. *Shema* is the first Hebrew word of the sentence, "Listen," which is also translated "Hear." The *shema* is a declaration of monotheism: There is one God who is consistent and never changes. The entire Bible stands on this theological foundation.

Moses' third address is dramatic. He describes the near future in which God will bless for obedience and punish for disobedience. He prophesies about a distant future in which Israel will disobey, be judged, and be scattered, but God will not give up on pursuing them.

Why God's Law Is Still Important Today

Christians today no longer adhere to the sacrificial system prescribed in the Old Testament because Christ fulfilled the requirements of the law when he died for us on the cross. "The law was our guardian until Christ came," writes the apostle Paul. "It protected us until we could be made right with God through faith" (Galatians 3:24). And yet, the law is still essential and relevant. We cannot understand our need for a Savior unless we grasp our own fallenness and brokenness. The law is revealing; it shows what is broken.

Paul also writes, "It was the law that showed me my sin" (Romans 7:7). And that is the purpose of the law—to expose the problem of sin. But the law cannot save us from our sin. Just as an X-ray exposes where a bone is broken but cannot heal the wound, God's law exposes the brokenness of sin but cannot heal it. The purpose of the covenant of grace in the New Testament is to complete the plan of salvation that began with the covenant of the law in the Old Testament.

Israel's History

A Story of Promise and Exile

THE HISTORICAL NARRATIVES in the Bible are factual, but they are not neutral. They are told from God's perspective. The historical books contain both the narrative of Israel's story and the ways in which God revealed himself through them. They include seven books: Joshua, Judges, Ruth, 1 and 2 Samuel, and 1 and 2 Kings. The books begin with a torrent of successes as Joshua leads the Israelites in the conquest of the Promised Land. The walls of Jericho fall and the blessings of God are poured out on his chosen people.

The story of Israel begins with so much promise! The book of Joshua is named after Israel's Promised Land leader, and it demonstrates the value of obedience. Judges records the people's subsequent steep descent into hopelessness. Religious compromise pulls the people away from God, and the effects of sin undermine Joshua's victories. Ruth is a grand story about God's sovereignty and the perseverance of faithful individuals living in a society that has fallen away from God. The books of 1 and 2 Samuel record the early history of Israel's first monarchy under Saul and David, while 1 and 2 Kings record the reign of Solomon and the fall of Jerusalem. As the story in 2 Kings closes, King Nebuchadnezzar of Babylon has invaded the land of Judah and destroyed the Temple in Jerusalem. Many of the Hebrew people are taken captive and exiled in various places throughout the Babylonian empire.

Though history records past events, the narratives in the Bible are also intended to give meaning to the present. The promises in the Old Testament are yours as a believer. As you read, remember that God is the hero of the story, and the events described show us what happens when we are faithful or unfaithful to the hero of the biblical story. The history recorded in the Old Testament is a grand narrative that reveals God's plan of redemption century after century and through various authors and characters. The individual stories within God's greater history are often complex and can be challenging to understand. Each story contains a narrator, a setting, and several characters. The narrator has a particular point of view. The setting involves a historical context. The characters are often described as contrasts to one another, such as Saul and David, Sanballat and Nehemiah, or Belshazzar and Daniel.

As you read the historical narratives of the Bible, it's important to note that the original text, though written, was meant to be spoken and heard. At the time, most people were unable to read. Therefore, God's Word was read aloud so the people could understand it. Those who wrote the dialogue between characters did so to convey the main point of the story. As part of that, they sometimes repeated words or phrases for emphasis. Also, the historical narratives record what happened, not necessarily what *should* have happened. As such, some stories are *descriptive* rather than *prescriptive*. Most of the characters in the Old Testament are deeply flawed, and many of the stories highlight what *not* to do as much as they point to what we should do.

The historical narratives are not comprehensive, which means they often leave out details. For example, major developments among other nations are often omitted from the recounting of Israel's history—which Old Testament scholar Eugene Merrill describes as a "cul-de-sac totally removed from the turbulent course of world events."[1] The Holy Spirit intended it this way. Every event in Israel's history is meant to point to God. Nothing in the Bible is a distraction from God. The historical record of Israel is a captivating story of God as the hero in salvation history.

Joshua: The Value of Obedience

When Moses transitions leadership to Joshua, Israel is ending forty years of wandering and is about to enter the Promised Land. During the forty years in the desert, Joshua had been Moses' faithful apprentice. Joshua first appeared in Exodus 17, when he led Israel to victory over the Amalekites. He was at the foot of Mount Sinai when Moses received the law. He was one of the twelve spies Moses sent on a reconnaissance mission to Canaan. Both he and Caleb urged their fellow Israelites to take the land by faith, but the other spies were afraid and convinced the people to wait.

Joshua is often viewed as a type of Christ. He has the same name—*Jesus* in Greek is a form of the Hebrew name Joshua. Much as Joshua led the people into the Promised Land, so, too, Jesus leads us into the promise of eternity with him in heaven. Joshua helped deliver people from the wilderness of disobedience. Jesus offers us the same deliverance from the wilderness of sin.

Joshua must help a new generation—the descendants of former

slaves—conquer Canaan, God's Promised Land. The events in the book span about twenty years. The narrative looks back and echoes the events of Exodus. The people must cross a body of water, this time the Jordan River, and God once again holds back the waters as he did when the people crossed the Red Sea forty years earlier.

In addition, the language of Joshua's farewell address is similar to that of Moses' farewell address. But the narrative of Joshua also looks forward and brings hope to the people after decades of wandering in the desert. Much of the book is conveyed through eyewitness accounts, perhaps written by Joshua's own hand (Joshua 24:26). The repeated phrase "to this day" indicates a time lapse between actual events and the writing of the book itself.

As with many books of the Bible, there are various ways to view the structure of the story. This simple outline highlights three key events as God's people enter the Promised Land:

Israel Conquers the Land (Joshua 1–12)

Israel Divides the Land (Joshua 13–21)

Israel Settles the Land (Joshua 22–24)

How did Israel conquer the land? First, God sovereignly desired for them to live there. When they obeyed him, he blessed their efforts. Second, no superpower like Egypt existed in the area at the time. Various cities and territories had their own kings. Israel was a smaller nation but had the ability to conquer these territories one at a time. As you read the middle section about dividing the land, the narrative is tedious and slow, much like the law narratives in Exodus. But this portion of Scripture is important because it demonstrates the fulfillment of God's promise to Abraham that his offspring would inherit the land.

Perhaps the best-known story in Joshua is that of Rahab and the fall of Jericho. Rahab, a prostitute, hides two Israelite spies when they arrive in Jericho and gives them critical intelligence about the city. God rewards her by sparing her and her household when the city falls. Rahab's life demonstrates how God's grace reaches all who humble themselves before him. God not only made her a leading character in Israel's victory over Jericho, he also included her in the lineage of Jesus (Matthew 1:5).

In Joshua 6, Jericho falls, but only after the Israelites follow God's directions precisely. In what seems like a ridiculous plan, the people walk around the city for seven days and then blow trumpets. By God's power, the walls of the city crumble. In this case, no military action is required. An important principle emerges that applies as much to our lives today as it did to God's people then: God's power minus our abilities equals total victory.

The book closes with Joshua's death at age 110. The final tribute to his leadership is something every Christian leader should seek: "The people of Israel served the LORD throughout the lifetime of Joshua" (Joshua 24:31). We do not need to understand everything God does in order to live faithfully. Like Joshua, we can experience victory when we let God fight on our behalf.

Judges: The Hopelessness of Compromise

The value of obedience in Joshua gives way to the hopelessness of compromise in Judges. Following the death of Joshua, Israel enters a dark age. The Hebrew people do not remain faithful to God, and he judges them. Though the book does contain judgment, its name is derived from a series of mostly failed military leaders—known as judges—who attempt to lead Israel during this time.

Judges is a transitional book, covering two to three hundred years of Israel's history. The successes under Joshua become a string of failures under several of the judges. There are also different kinds of leaders in the time of the judges. Some are charismatic military leaders, such as Samson. Some are priests, such as Eli. Others are prophets, such as Deborah and Samuel. They rule in different regions and are not in charge of the nation of Israel as a whole. In fact, no central authority exists in Israel during this period because the people do not recognize God's leadership and the monarchy has yet to be established. During this era, Israel continually sins against God. The book of Judges is not chronological but functions more as a collection of stories on the theme of Israel's lack of faithfulness. The author of the book is unknown, though Jewish tradition points to the prophet Samuel.

God wants his people to settle in the land he promised to them. He desires to provide a home for them. Yet, after four hundred years of slavery and four decades of wandering in the wilderness, they still struggle with obeying God's commands.

Of the judges, six stand out because of the cycle of moral failure contained in their stories. A pattern emerges. Israel compromises and falls into sin, typically by worshiping other gods. God then exercises his anger and allows Israel's enemies to oppress them. The people cry out in distress, and God rescues them through a judge. When the judge dies, a new cycle of failure begins.

Passage	Judge	Enemy
Judges 3:7-11	Othniel	Mesopotamians
Judges 3:12-30	Ehud	Moabites and Ammonites
Judges 4:1–5:31	Deborah	Canaanites
Judges 6:1–8:35	Gideon	Midianites
Judges 10:6–12:7	Jephthah	Ammonites
Judges 13:1–16:31	Samson	Philistines

UNDERSTANDING THE BIBLE AS A WHOLE

The book begins, "After the death of Joshua" (Judges 1:1). This first verse marks a notable theological transition as a period of conquest under Joshua becomes a period of judgment because the people have not obeyed God completely and have not driven out all the Canaanites. The remaining Canaanites plague the Israelites throughout the book. The judges God appoints are not necessarily the best leaders, but they illustrate the persistence of God's grace and mercy.

Chapters 17 through 21 function as an appendix that documents the lawlessness of the nation of Israel. Here we read of idolatry, war, conspiracy, senseless violence, and sexual deviance. Israel in the book of Judges demonstrates how a society can self-destruct. The closing verse of the final chapter indicates the real tragedy: "All the people did whatever seemed right in their own eyes" (Judges 21:25). Unchecked sin always ends in destruction.

Ruth: A Bright Spot of Faithfulness

During the spiritually dark time of the judges, the story of Ruth is a bright spot. While Judges focuses on broad stories about the leadership of the entire nation, Ruth tells a story about specific and ordinary people. The main characters are not kings, judges, or prophets, but commoners. Moreover, Ruth is both a woman and a widow. She has no power and no wealth. She is a single woman and a refugee, barely scraping by in a time of famine. And yet, she is one of only two women to have a book in the Bible named for them. The other is Esther. Additionally, Ruth is one of only five women named in the lineage of Jesus in Matthew 1.

The author of the book is unknown, but in four short chapters a beautiful narrative emerges that is one of the finest examples of literature anywhere.

Ruth's Friendship with Naomi (Ruth 1)

Ruth's Meeting with Boaz (Ruth 2)

Ruth's Proposal for Marriage (Ruth 3)

Ruth's Reward for Faithfulness (Ruth 4)

To escape a severe famine in Israel, a man named Elimelech and his wife, Naomi, along with their two sons, travel to Moab from their home of Bethlehem. They are Israelites, but the two sons grow up to marry Moabite women. When Elimelech and both of his sons die, Naomi and her daughters-in-law, Ruth and Orpah, are left as widows. Naomi decides to go back to Bethlehem, and Orpah returns to her family home in Moab—but Ruth does not. Instead, she returns to Bethlehem with Naomi and chooses to follow the God of Israel.

Naomi is bitter because of her losses, but Ruth serves her faithfully by gleaning crops, a practice permitted for the poor. When the landowner Boaz hears of Ruth's service to Naomi, he instructs his workers to leave grain behind for her. Naomi repays Ruth's kindness by devising a plan to prompt Boaz to take Ruth as his wife. After a bold nighttime encounter at the threshing floor, Boaz decides to marry Ruth. Eventually, they have a son, Obed, who later will become the grandfather of King David.

This story is remarkable. Even the title of the book is noteworthy. Ruth is not an Israelite but a Moabite. Hers is the only Old Testament book named after a non-Israelite. A key theme of the book is that God alone can bring fulfillment out of emptiness. The story begins with the tragedy of loss, but God moves the characters to a better place in a way that can only be attributed to him. Ruth's story in Bethlehem foreshadows a New Testament event that also takes place in Bethlehem; namely, the birth of Jesus. Boaz emerges as a kinsman-redeemer, one who "had the privilege or responsibility to act for a relative who was in trouble, danger, or need of vindication."[2] In redeeming Ruth, Boaz becomes a picture of the coming Messiah. The story begins in tragedy but ends in redemption and delight.

1 and 2 Samuel: Triumph and Troubles

Following the tumultuous period of the judges, the people demand a king. The books of 1 and 2 Samuel tell the early history of Israel's monarchy under Saul and David. While 1 Samuel covers events that span more than a hundred years, 2 Samuel covers only the forty years of David's reign. The narrative begins with the prophet Samuel, the last of the judges. Though 1 and 2 Samuel have an unattributed author, the eyewitness accounts in 1 Samuel suggest that the prophet himself wrote at least a portion of the book. As 1 Samuel begins, Israel is struggling with an identity crisis. Many nations around Israel are also declining, but the Philistines are on the rise. The Philistines are not prominent in the total scope of world history, but they pester the Israelites throughout the time period recorded in these books. Israel's solution to the problems is simple, or so they believe. They want a king of their own.

The narrative structure of 1 Samuel follows three primary characters:

Samuel, the Last of the Judges (1 Samuel 1–8)

Saul, the First of the Kings (1 Samuel 8–15)

David, God's Chosen Leader (1 Samuel 16–31)

God grants his people's request for a king, but it is not his ideal plan for them. The Hebrew people want to be led by a human being rather than by God. As both a judge and a prophet, Samuel wants the people to trust God, but they persist in their demands for a king. Saul is admired by the people, perhaps because he looks like a king—handsome and standing "head and shoulders taller than anyone else in the land" (1 Samuel 9:2). God wants to maintain his place of authority over the people, but he allows them their king. Here we learn an important lesson: We can either seek to please God's heart or please our own—with all the consequences that will ensue. Choosing God's *direct* will is always better than choosing his *permissive* will. We should not want only what God will *permit* but rather what will *delight* him.

Saul has some initial military successes, but disobedience and sin soon undermine his rule. He usurps the priestly role when it serves his purposes. He makes a rash oath and applies it in a foolish way. He fails to follow God's instructions concerning the Amalekites. He is impatient and acts impulsively. In the end, he dies by suicide in a battle against the Philistines after a downward spiral into sin.

At God's directive, Samuel anoints a teenager, David, as Israel's new king (1 Samuel 16), though David will not take the throne until after Saul's death, a gap of about fifteen years. David is chosen because of his heart, not his stature. After killing Goliath, David is catapulted into fame. He becomes good friends with Saul's son Jonathan and goes to great lengths to prove his loyalty. The narrative of 1 Samuel is rife with the tension between Saul and David, driven largely by Saul's jealousy. The theme of both 1 and 2 Samuel is one of triumph turned to trouble through the consequences of sin.

When 2 Samuel opens, David officially takes the throne. He is thirty years old and will reign for forty years. Upon Saul's death, David's tribe (Judah) in the southern part of the kingdom declares him king, whereas the northern tribes acknowledge Saul's youngest son, Ishbosheth, as their king. It will be another seven years before the southern and northern tribes are united and David becomes king over all of Israel. Under David, Jerusalem is named as the capital of Israel. He brings the Ark of the Covenant, constructed according to the pattern given at Mt. Sinai, to Jerusalem, and he desires to build a permanent Temple to house the Ark.

The narrative structure of 2 Samuel falls into two parts:

David's Triumphs and God's Blessings (2 Samuel 1–10)

David's Troubles and God's Judgment (2 Samuel 11–24)

David's triumphs, much like those of Saul, eventually turn to trouble. David's sin with Bathsheba destroys two families, and the consequences reverberate throughout the kingdom. The big difference between David and Saul is *repentance*. Unlike Saul, after David rebels, he acknowledges his sin, repents, and returns to God. The Psalms record many of David's most gut-wrenching moments of repentance and remorse. Both 1 and 2 Samuel are precursors of the New Testament theme that God's grace is sufficient to cover all sins of those who recognize his holiness and return to him in repentance.

1 and 2 Kings: Division and Collapse

The once robust kingdom under David begins to deteriorate under the leadership of his son, Solomon. The kingdom splits in two, and several evil kings follow in Solomon's wake. The Hebrew people are conquered and scattered into exile. Together, 1 and 2 Kings account for events covering approximately four hundred years (one hundred years in 1 Kings, three hundred years in 2 Kings).

The author analyzes the succession of kings through the lens of their obedience to God. Some of the low points include the apostasy of Ahab, Ahaz, and Manasseh. Some of the highlights include the religious reforms of Jehu, Hezekiah, and Josiah. The purpose is to evaluate how leaders were loyal to God and then detail the national consequences of disloyalty to God. Ultimately, the people are kicked out of the Promised Land because of their rebellion.

The small nation of Israel had risen to prominence as God blessed their obedience under King David, but their success turns to failure under Solomon as he falls into sin. During Solomon's reign, Israel is influential in the region but eventually splits into the southern kingdom of Judah and the northern kingdom of Israel. The era is marked by political successes, but also spiritual failures.

The authorship of 1 and 2 Kings is unknown. Jewish tradition points to Jeremiah, but there is no claim of authorship in the books themselves. First Kings records the unwinding of the Davidic kingdom, and 2 Kings records the collapse of the nation as both Judah and Israel fall into captivity. It is a dreary period in the history of God's people. The Assyrians destroy the northern kingdom of Israel. The Babylonians destroy the southern kingdom of Judah. The following chart provides a brief overview of both kingdoms.

Israel (Northern Kingdom)	Judah (Southern Kingdom)
Ten tribes	Two tribes
Capital: Samaria	Capital: Jerusalem
Conquered 722 BC	Conquered 587 BC
Conquered by the Assyrians	Conquered by the Babylonians

The structure of 1 and 2 Kings follows the rise and fall of Israel into a divided nation and a conquered people.

Solomon's Forty-Year Reign and a Kingdom United
   (1 Kings 1–11)

The First Eighty Years of a Kingdom Divided
   (1 Kings 12–22)

Events in the Northern Kingdom of Israel
   (2 Kings 1–10)

Events in Both Kingdoms (2 Kings 11–17)

Events in the Southern Kingdom of Judah
   (2 Kings 18–25)

Solomon reigns about forty years. The spoils from his father's wars enable him to build the Jerusalem Temple. Like his father, Solomon is a prolific writer. While David composed many of the psalms and hymns included in the book of Psalms, Solomon composed many of the wisdom sayings in the book of Proverbs. Though Solomon enjoys some early civic successes driven by his desire for God's wisdom, they do not last. Under the influence of his many foreign wives, Solomon turns to other gods and leads Israel from monotheism to polytheism.

Following Solomon's death and the loss of the united kingdom, a string of evil kings lead the northern kingdom of Israel and the southern kingdom of Judah further away from God. The prophets Elijah and Elisha arrive on the scene and speak out against the evil taking place in Israel. Other prophets speaking during this time include Obadiah, Joel, Micah, Isaiah, Nahum, Habakkuk, Zephaniah, and Jeremiah. Through dozens of kings over the course of hundreds of years, the same theme emerges again and again: Willful disobedience leads to division among God's people.

The Greatest History Lesson

The greatest lesson of history is straightforward. God is the hero. Just like the characters in the Bible, we will succeed or fail based on our view of God. Scripture reveals God's plan of redemption to save his wayward people. The historical books of the Bible only make sense if God is the supreme character. It is tempting to read ourselves into the stories of the Bible. Indeed, it's good to learn personal lessons from Scripture, as we will see in Proverbs, but the only way to discern how to live properly is to place God above everything and everyone else. The historical books demonstrate what happens when we rebel against God, and they also reveal God's blessings when we live in obedience to him. God made a covenant with Abraham and promised to give him land. God made a covenant with David and promised him a throne. These historical works answer an unavoidable question: Why did the tragedy of destruction and exile occur? God didn't fail his people. They failed him.

4

The Post-exilic Period

A Remnant Returns to Jerusalem

SOLOMON'S TEMPLE AND the city of Jerusalem were destroyed by King Nebuchadnezzar and the Babylonians. Around 604 BC, the Hebrew people were forced into Babylonian exile. Sixty-six years later, Babylon fell to the Persian army. Cyrus, the ruler who conquered Babylon, allowed the Hebrew exiles to return home in 538 BC. Many of the Hebrew people actually chose to remain in exile, but a few ventured back to their beloved homeland. What they found was a city in ruins. And so they began a vast rebuilding effort. This period in the history of God's people is referred to as the post-exilic era. The post-exilic books include 1 and 2 Chronicles, Ezra, Nehemiah, and Esther.

The return of the exiles happened in two waves, the first of which was led by Zerubbabel, the Judean governor who oversaw the rebuilding of the Temple. The work was challenging. Several adversaries who lived in the area surrounding Jerusalem did not want the city to rise in power again, and they attempted to stop the reconstruction. But Cyrus allowed the work to continue. Materials were difficult to obtain, and the new Temple was not as ornate as Solomon's Temple. After the initial fervor that surrounded the rebuilding, the people's excitement waned.

The post-exilic era was one of many highs and lows. The resettling of Jerusalem and the rebuilding of the Temple meant the sacrificial system could be reinstated. God's promises about the land of Canaan were still valid, and the people could again sense the Lord's blessings. However, they continued to struggle with the same sins that had sent them into captivity in the first place, and God continued to send prophets to challenge the people to remain holy. In telling the story of reconstructing their nation, writers of the post-exilic books used genealogies to demonstrate the connections between God's people and the patriarchs of their past.[1] God's covenant remained. He never swayed from his promises.

After Zerubbabel, the second wave of exiles to return was led by Ezra, a priest and scribe. Ezra was instrumental in restoring the sacrificial system and reestablishing worship in the Temple. Not only did Ezra help with the physical rebuilding projects, he also taught the people about God's law and the path of obedience. Nehemiah returned as well and led an effort to rebuild the walls surrounding Jerusalem. Esther was a member of the Jewish community who chose to stay in exile rather than return to the holy city. When her people were threatened with genocide, Esther embarked on a daring mission to rescue them. As the post-exilic books conclude, the hopelessness and division of the era recorded in the historical books begins to fade as the Jewish people unite to rebuild the Temple and the city of Jerusalem.

1 and 2 Chronicles: Reminders of God's Promises

Both 1 and 2 Chronicles function as commentaries on other texts, and they are the first of their kind in Scripture. Just as Bible commentaries today analyze and explain the meaning of various Scriptures, 1 and 2 Chronicles examine and comment on portions of 1 and 2 Samuel and 1 and 2 Kings.

Judging by the genealogies in 1 and 2 Chronicles, they were probably written during the second or third generation after the Exile ended, between 450 BC and 400 BC. Originally one book, they were later divided into two: 1 Chronicles covers the death of Saul and David's reign (1 and 2 Samuel), while 2 Chronicles covers Solomon's reign (1 and 2 Kings).

Genealogies (1 Chronicles 1–9)

Reign of David (1 Chronicles 10–29)

Reign of Solomon (2 Chronicles 1–9)

Kingdom of Judah (2 Chronicles 10–36)

The chronicler is unknown, though some attribute the books to the prophet Ezra. First Chronicles begins with a long string of genealogies, but don't overlook them. These records are critically important. Just as we enjoy tracing our roots through tools such as Ancestry.com, the Jewish people wanted to know their heritage. The genealogies show how God sovereignly preserved them through the tragedy of exile and remained faithful to his covenant.

These historical books are considered post-exilic literature because of when and why they were written. Though the Exile has ended, God's people are still reeling from the consequences of being subjugated by the Babylonians and the Assyrians. Poverty is rampant, and Jerusalem is in ruins. Many Hebrews are still scattered far from their homeland. Has God forsaken his people? No, he has not, and the chronicler wants to remind the Jews of God's faithfulness. The writer looks back and traces God's promises throughout their history to reassure the people they have not been forgotten.

In the Christian canon, the post-exilic books are situated after 1 and 2 Kings but before Ezra and Nehemiah. In the Jewish canon, they come last. One reason for this is that the Jews wanted to conclude the Old Testament on a high note. Because the writer wants to affirm God's faithfulness and promises, certain stories about the people's lack of faithfulness are omitted from 1 and 2 Chronicles. Israel's many failures are conspicuously absent. David's sin with Bathsheba is not mentioned, nor is the attempt of his sons to usurp the throne. The text includes quotes from Solomon recorded in 1 Kings, but it makes no reference to Solomon's apostasy. The selectivity is intentional. At this point in Israel's history, the people are well aware of their failures. Indeed, they are living the consequences of their sin. The chronicler is not attempting to rewrite history; rather, he is trying to focus on how God's promises have remained valid throughout the nation's history. The ending points to hope. Second Chronicles closes with the edict of Cyrus the Persian, which sets the people free. God is beginning to restore his people to the land he originally promised them.

Ezra: Rebuilding the Temple

The books of Ezra and Nehemiah are often studied together. In the Jewish canon, they are combined into one book, and they record contemporaneous historical narratives. A compiler used the memoirs of Ezra and Nehemiah, as well as other historical narratives, to offer a high-level view of the rebuilding efforts led by Zerubbabel and Ezra.

The Return of Zerubbabel (Ezra 1–6)

The Return of Ezra (Ezra 7–10)

In the first part of Ezra, Zerubbabel, the grandson of King Jehoiachin, provides political leadership to kick-start the rebuilding of Jerusalem. The foundation of the Temple is laid. When the people face opposition, they stop working and leave the Temple unfinished. For sixteen years, they neglect God's work and focus instead on rebuilding their own homes. The prophets Haggai and Zechariah provide the spiritual push to restart the work, which begins under Ezra's leadership. Note the parallels between the two waves of returning exiles, first under Zerubbabel and then under Ezra.[2]

Return under Zerubbabel (Ezra 1–6)	Return under Ezra (Ezra 7–10)
The decree of Cyrus (Ezra 1:1-4)	The decree of Artaxerxes (Ezra 7:11-26)
The leader Zerubbabel (Ezra 2:2)	The leader Ezra (Ezra 7:1-10)
Names and number of the remnant (Ezra 2:3-65)	Names and number of the company (Ezra 8:1-20)
The coming to Jerusalem (Ezra 3:1)	The coming to Jerusalem (Ezra 8:32)
Prophetic ministry of Haggai and Zechariah (Ezra 5:1; 6:14)	Intercessory ministry of Ezra (Ezra 9:1-15)
The Temple is rebuilt (Ezra 6:15-22)	The nation is rebuilt (Ezra 10:1-44)

After the Temple is rebuilt, King Artaxerxes of Persia authorizes another group of Jews to return to Jerusalem under Ezra's leadership. As a priest, Ezra provides spiritual leadership to the returning exiles, just as Haggai and Zechariah had done under Zerubbabel.

When Ezra discovers that the Jewish people have intermarried with other nations, he calls for repentance. The issue is idolatry. The other nations serve other gods, which leads to syncretism—the merging of differing beliefs into one system. By mixing religious practices, the Jewish people were once again compromising their purity and having an identity crisis. Ezra initiates reforms and sets the stage for the next part of the story, the reconstruction of the walls surrounding Jerusalem.

Nehemiah: Reconstructing the Wall

Though others, such as Haggai and Zerubbabel, returned to Jerusalem to rebuild their homes and lay the foundation for restoring the Temple, Nehemiah returns to help rebuild the city walls. The book of Nehemiah opens with the arrival of bad news in the Jewish month of Chislev, which is November and December on the Gregorian calendar we use today. Nehemiah, an exile residing in Persia, gets a disturbing message from Hanani, a close friend or likely his biological brother. The few people left in Jerusalem are in trouble, and the city is in ruins. This is devastating news as the hope of rebuilding the city fades and the ruins remain. After an agonizing prayer, Nehemiah realizes that God is calling him to return to Jerusalem. He leaves his high-ranking position under the king of Persia to restore the walls of Jerusalem.

A two-part problem emerges in the book of Nehemiah, which is reflected in the book's structure. The walls must be rebuilt, and the people must be retaught to honor God.

Work on the Walls (Nehemiah 1–6)

Work on the People (Nehemiah 7–13)

City walls are a necessary defense against foreign invaders, but the walls also symbolize how God wants to secure the purity of his people. With everyone working together under Nehemiah's leadership, the walls are rebuilt in just over seven weeks.

This book provides a great example of the challenges and rewards of serving God. Nehemiah was called to lead the Jewish people to rebuild the walls of Jerusalem. As they work, they encounter opposition and ridicule from their enemies, but they persist because they have prioritized God's work. At one point, the people turn on each other during the rebuilding project, and they are tempted to quit. But Nehemiah helps them understand that finishing the task is essential because God's name is at stake.

Through their service, Nehemiah and the people realize that more than just physical walls are being built. God also uses their work to rebuild them spiritually. They read God's Word together and then have a giant celebration after the walls are completed. Thus, the work is just as much about rebuilding them as God's people as it was about rebuilding the walls of Jerusalem.

Esther: Rescuing the Exiles

The last of the post-exilic books is a short narrative and romantic drama written by an unknown author. A remnant of Jewish people has returned to Jerusalem while the vast majority remain in exile. Esther is the story of an orphaned Jewish girl in exile who becomes the queen of the Persian Empire through the sovereignty of God. She uses her position to save her people from annihilation. The time frame of her story falls between the events recorded in Ezra 6 and 7.

Historical events connect the books of Ezra, Nehemiah, and Esther, but the narratives also reveal contrasting elements. Though the history they record is consistent, the three books have different genres, styles, settings, and purposes.

	Ezra/Nehemiah	Esther
Genre	Historical records	Artful narrative
Style	Royal edicts and memoirs	Dialogue and elaborate plot
Setting	Religious	Secular
Purpose	Return to Jerusalem	Remain in exile

Four main characters carry the plot in the book of Esther. The Persian king Xerxes is a ruler whose arrogance contrasts with the humility God demands. The villain is a foreigner to Persia named Haman, who has elevated himself to the second-most powerful position, just under the king. The Jewish protagonist is Mordecai, who also serves in the king's court. Mordecai's younger cousin, Esther, is the brave and winsome heroine who saves an entire group of God's people.

When Queen Vashti defends her honor and refuses to appear at a drunken party hosted by King Xerxes, he banishes her and begins to look for a new queen. After an elaborate search, he chooses Esther. Meanwhile, Mordecai uncovers a plot to kill the king, and he tells Esther, who relays the message to her husband.

A parallel story emerges between Mordecai and Haman. After appointing Haman over all the other nobles, King Xerxes decrees that all of his officials should bow down when Haman passes by. When Mordecai refuses, Haman is enraged. Out of spite, Haman forms a plan to exterminate not only Mordecai but the entire Jewish population. Haman deceives the king into issuing an edict to kill all the Jews (which includes Esther, but the king is not aware of her heritage).

When Mordecai discovers the plot, he challenges Esther to use her position to intervene with the king: "Who knows if perhaps you were made queen for just such a time as this?" (Esther 4:14).

Knowing she risks her life by approaching the king without being summoned, Esther nevertheless invites the king to a banquet where she plans to expose Haman's wicked plan. The night before the banquet, the king is unable to sleep and asks that his royal archives be read to him. This is when he learns that Mordecai has never been rewarded for exposing the plot to kill him.

The next morning, Xerxes asks Haman how he should reward a hero. Thinking he himself is the hero in question, Haman suggests a lavish public ceremony. The king loves Haman's plan and promptly puts him in charge of bestowing the reward on Mordecai. Esther then exposes Haman's genocidal plan. King Xerxes has Haman hanged and issues a new edict protecting the Jews. All are saved, and Mordecai becomes the new prime minister.

The book of Esther is a literary masterpiece. The structure follows the significant events of the plotline.

Vashti Rejected (Esther 1)

Esther Chosen (Esther 2)

Haman's Selfish Plot (Esther 3–4)

Esther's Selfless Risk (Esther 5)

The Jews Delivered (Esther 6–10)

The characters in the story come alive, and the narrative engages the reader from start to finish. Amazingly, God's name is never mentioned in the book. Yet he is the central character. His sovereign hand guides Esther throughout the story. God preserves the Jewish people using a pagan king and a daring young woman. The book of Esther reminds us that even when God seems silent, he is working.

The Reward of Faithfulness

Esther remained in exile, but she was faithful. Her faithfulness protected God's people. Nehemiah left his lucrative position for the difficult task of rebuilding Jerusalem, but he was faithful. His faithfulness helped defend God's people. Ezra challenged the people with an unpopular message, but he was faithful. His faithfulness preserved God's people. The chronicler reminded the Jews that the highlights of their history occurred when they were faithful. The post-exilic books are important because they record a specific time of Israel's history, but their greatest purpose is to reveal the rewards of remaining faithful to the one true God.

Poetry and Wisdom

Humanity's Vital Connection to God

THE BIBLE APPEALS not only to what we should *know* but also to what we *feel*. Human emotion derives from God himself. As creatures made in God's image, we have emotions because he has emotions. The Bible is, in a sense, an emotional love letter from God to his people, and it captures humanity's emotional response to God—especially in the five books of poetry and wisdom: Job, Psalms, Proverbs, Ecclesiastes, and Song of Songs.[1]

The first seventeen books of the Bible—encompassing the law, the early history of Israel, and the post-exilic books of prophecy—focus on the condition of Israel as a nation. The next five books of poetry and wisdom literature focus on the human heart. Scripture includes expressions of human praise, angst, joy, sorrow, and solace. Virtually every human emotion finds expression in the poetry of the Bible. The books of poetry are also considered *wisdom* literature because of the emphasis they place on under-standing every aspect of human life.

In this chapter, we'll cover four of the five poetry and wisdom books, and then devote an entire chapter to the Psalms.

As you read the poetic books in the Bible, it is important to note some characteristics of Hebrew poetry. The most obvious is that the poems in the Old Testament were written in Hebrew, not English. Most translations attempt to keep the poetic flow of the original language, but not every creative element translates clearly into English. For example, poems in Scripture rely more on meter than rhyme. Therefore, the translators emphasize the cadence rather than trying to make the couplets rhyme, as we might do in English. A popular form of poetry in the Bible is the acrostic, in which each verse of the poem begins with a different letter of the Hebrew alphabet. Both Psalm 119 and Proverbs 31 are notable acrostics.

The chief characteristic of Hebrew poetry is parallelism, a poetic style in which two lines of verse complement each other. Parallelism translates easily into other languages "without concern for rhyme or meter."[2] Bible scholar Norman Geisler identifies four common types of parallelism in Scripture: *synonymous, antithetical, synthetical,* and *exemplar.*[3]

Synonymous parallelism repeats the same thought. The word *and* is often the key to synonymous parallelism. For example:

The heavens tell of the glory of God;
and their expanse declares the work of His hands.
PSALM 19:1, NASB

Antithetical parallelism contrasts two lines with opposing views. With antithetical parallelism, *but* is the key word.

The life of the godly is full of light and joy,
> but the light of the wicked will be snuffed out.

PROVERBS 13:9

Synthetical parallelism occurs when the second line develops the thought in the first line. With synthetical parallelism, the words *but* and *and* are typically absent.

The king's fury is like a lion's roar;
> to rouse his anger is to risk your life.

PROVERBS 20:2

In exemplar parallelism, "one line metaphorically illustrates the literal truth of the other."[4]

As iron sharpens iron,
> so a friend sharpens a friend.

PROVERBS 27:17

Look for these characteristics as you read passages in the poetry books. They offer clues about the purpose of the text, reveal the author's artistic skill, and help readers connect emotionally to God's Word—one of the most important qualities of biblical poetry, especially in the Psalms.

Job: The Reality of Suffering

One of the oldest books of the Bible goes right to the heart of one of humanity's most enduring questions: *Why do godly people suffer?* Written by an unknown author, the book of Job records the story of a man who lived during the time of the Patriarchs in Genesis. This man, Job, was not only wealthy and powerful but also righteous.

The book opens with a fascinating scene—a dialogue between Satan and God. Satan claims that God's followers are righteous only because of God's blessings, not because they love God for who he is. To prove his point, Satan secures God's permission to attack Job.

In the first of two attacks, Satan targets Job's wealth and his family. Satan wipes out Job's cattle, sheep, camels, and servants, and then murders his children. Instead of cursing God, Job praises God, even in the midst of his profound grief and loss. In the second attack, Satan targets Job's health, leaving him deathly sick. At this point, even Job's wife tells him to "curse God and die," as a means to end the pain (Job 2:9). Job refuses. While his wife blames God for Job's troubles, Job's friends blame *him*. Job gives voice to his intense pain as he cries out that he is cut off from God.

The structure of the book reveals the flow of the story.

Opening Scene with God, Satan, and Job (Job 1–2)

Dialogues with Job's Friends (Job 3–27)

Middle Discourse on Wisdom (Job 28)

Monologues from Job, Elihu, and God (Job 29–41)

Closing Scene and God's Restoration of Job (Job 42)

A long poem, encompassing a series of dialogues, begins in Job 3 and continues into the last chapter. Five speakers try to discern why Job suffers. The first three—Eliphaz, Bildad, and Zophar—oversimplify Job's sufferings and base their conclusions on their own understanding. They believe that if Job will own up to his sin, God will restore him. Job refutes their conclusions that only the wicked suffer and only the righteous prosper. Yet he struggles to provide an explanation for his own suffering. He knows God has allowed his suffering, and he also knows there is no sin in his life that corresponds to the severity of his suffering. Job cannot confess sins he has not committed. These first three dialogues with Eliphaz, Bildad, and Zophar grow progressively shorter as everyone runs out of things to say.

Two more monologues follow, beginning in Job 29. Job and his friend Elihu discuss more potential explanations for his suffering. Finally, in Job 38, God himself speaks. He ends his silence with a loud whirlwind. One of the more difficult aspects of the poem is that God's response offers neither explanation nor comfort. Instead, he presses Job for answers, essentially saying, "Who are you, Job? And who am I?" For four chapters, God details his complete power. By the end of God's speech, Job is finally satisfied and no longer demands an explanation. He is comforted by who God is, rather than by what God can provide. "Surely I spoke of things I did not understand," he says, "things too wonderful for me to know" (Job 42:3, NIV). Having seen God, Job realizes he will never understand everything, and states, "I take back everything I said" (Job 42:6).

Chief among the book's many lessons is that Satan can be defeated through our suffering. God used Job to defeat evil! We also learn that Satan's power has limits and that he is accountable to God. As the book ends, God redeems Job's suffering by restoring to him "twice as much as he had before" (Job 42:10, NIV).

We might still wonder why God allowed Job's suffering. Job himself proclaimed he was innocent and considered himself cut off from God. Though the text makes it clear that God himself considered Job "blameless—a man of complete integrity" (Job 1:8), Job was not totally innocent, because Job is not God. Ultimately, the message of the book points us to Christ, the only truly innocent sufferer who was temporarily cut off from God when he took on our sin. Job could not save himself. You and I cannot save ourselves. Only God can restore us.

Proverbs: Everyday Wisdom

A biblical proverb is a short statement of divine wisdom meant to be applied to everyday experiences. Where psalms are often emotional and devotional, proverbs are practical and action oriented.

The book of Proverbs contains more than nine hundred wise sayings, many of them written by Solomon. Unfortunately, though Solomon *wrote* about wisdom, he did not always live accordingly. Other authors in Proverbs include Hezekiah, King Lemuel and his mother, and Agur, as well as other wise commentators.

Proverbs are general wisdom principles. They help us make wise choices that establish a right pattern of living. The driving force behind this pattern of living is a healthy fear of God. Such fear is not equivalent to terror but to a reverent understanding of our true position before our Creator. We are to live knowing that God loves us, and he is constantly aware of every action and thought we have.

Though each proverb stands on its own, the book of Proverbs can be divided into three general sections.

Wisdom for the Young and Inexperienced (Proverbs 1–10)

Wisdom for All People (Proverbs 11–20)

Wisdom for Leaders (Proverbs 21–31)

The wisdom in Proverbs provides both insight and foresight. Insight correctly assesses a problem. Foresight creates an appropriate and effective solution to the problem. When we absorb the wisdom of proverbs, we learn how life works, we understand God's standards, and we grow in our ability to make meaningful connections between the two. Mere knowledge is not enough. We must know what to do with our knowledge. Wisdom is what helps us apply God's standards to real life.

Proverbs are wise principles, but they are not promises. Applying a proverb doesn't guarantee the outcome of a situation. For example, consider the familiar proverb, "Direct your children onto the right path, and when they are older, they will not leave it" (Proverbs 22:6). Though this is practical wisdom, it is not a promise that our children will always follow God's plan if we raise them properly. It is a statement of general truth but not a guarantee.

Proverbs are also general guidelines but not necessarily universal commands. For example, one proverb says, "Don't befriend angry people or associate with hot-tempered people" (Proverbs 22:24). The general principle is to be careful when choosing your friends because they will influence your character. This proverb doesn't mean we should *never* make friends with anyone who has a temper.

Proverbs acknowledges two different categories of unwise people: the inexperienced and the fools. The inexperienced are naive and typically young—those who tend to make decisions based on peer pressure. The inexperienced often choose what is popular over what is right because they are concerned about what others think. Fools are those who are wise in their own eyes. They make decisions based on what feels right to them in the moment. Fools don't care enough to learn wisdom or apply it. The overarching lesson is that it is dangerous to base your life decisions on what others think or on your own impulses and feelings.

Unfortunately, there is no quick fix for a lack of wisdom. Proverbs teaches that while foolishness comes naturally and instantaneously, wisdom is acquired slowly through applying God's Word.

The good news is that God lavishly bestows wisdom on those who seek it. "If you need wisdom, ask our generous God," writes the apostle James, "and he will give it to you" (James 1:5). The more than nine hundred poetic proverbs demonstrate that God values wisdom and desires to give us clear instructions for living well.

Ecclesiastes: Everything Is Empty Apart from God

Proverbs has a tidiness to its poetry. Each piece of wisdom stands on its own and is straightforward. By contrast, Ecclesiastes is messy. A teacher narrates the book. Though there is no claim of authorship, it was likely written by Solomon near the end of his life as he reflected on the consequences of straying from God's wisdom. Though God gifted Solomon with wisdom, and though Solomon recorded it faithfully, he often failed to apply it to his own life.

The book reflects on a time of Israel's despair as the kingdom is collapsing. The recurring theme is the emptiness of everything apart from God, and the meaninglessness of any preoccupation with material goods. Solomon finds no satisfaction in anything "under the sun" (Ecclesiastes 1:9). This phrase appears about twenty times in the book and is a continual reminder of the vanity of seeking purpose apart from God. In a loud lament, the teacher begins, "Everything is meaningless . . . completely meaningless!" (Ecclesiastes 1:2). The book comments on several pursuits, including philosophy, pleasure, and religion. All of them prove empty without God. The search for enjoyment produces nothing, and Ecclesiastes records the hollowness of a life devoid of God.

Ecclesiastes can be divided into four main sections.

The Emptiness of Personal Pursuits (Ecclesiastes 1–2)

The Emptiness of Human Activity (Ecclesiastes 3–5)

The Elusiveness of True Wisdom (Ecclesiastes 6–8)

Death: The Great Equalizer (Ecclesiastes 9–12)

The book opens in a deeply personal way as Solomon reflects on his own life in the first two chapters. Then, beginning in Ecclesiastes 3, he progresses into more general observations about humanity. Oppression and inequality seem to define the human condition. Even wealth and honor are ultimately meaningless as people turn to evil. A turning point occurs in Ecclesiastes 8, where Solomon acknowledges that the best path in life begins with fearing God:

> Even though a person sins a hundred times and still lives
> a long time, I know that those who fear God will be
> better off.
> ECCLESIASTES 8:12

The book concludes with a stark realization that death comes to all. The only hope we have is to acknowledge our Creator. The book is a warning for those who pursue pleasure without fearing God. In that sense, Ecclesiastes is unavoidably pessimistic. Just as the Psalms record some of David's gut-wrenching laments, Ecclesiastes records Solomon's epic poem of regret. The purpose of this book is not to undermine our hope but rather to allow us to learn from Solomon's despair and to remind us that only God gives meaning. Everything else will fade, but God never will.

Song of Songs: Celebrating Love in Marriage
An old tradition holds that Jewish men were discouraged from reading the Song of Songs until they were thirty years old. A quick perusal of the text reveals why. Song of Songs is a celebration of

love and sex between a married man and woman. This love poem is unique and full of evocative images. Some scholars believe the imagery is allegorical of Christ and his church, but it is better to take the book at face value. A husband and wife enjoy each other with no inhibitions.

Song of Songs is a series of love poems written back and forth between a husband and his wife. God is not mentioned in the book, but his design for intimacy in marriage is clear. The poem takes us back to the Garden of Eden before the Fall, when Adam and Eve were naked and felt no shame. Song of Songs is a passionate poem about the intimacy and fidelity of a husband and wife—the way God intends for marriage to be. A debate exists among scholars as to whether the man in the poem is Solomon. It is a possible interpretation, as there are references to "the king" in the series of poems. If Solomon is the author, then the book represents an early expression of his passion and desire, a stark contrast to the helplessness of his words in Ecclesiastes.

It's difficult to identify a clear thematic structure in these back-and-forth poems between the husband and wife. The chronology of the dialogue is difficult to ascertain. To identify the various speakers, many Bibles add subheads such as "he" or "young man" for the husband; "she" or "young woman" for the wife; and "young women of Jerusalem," "friends," or even "others" for various other speakers and narrators. The one thing that's clear in this beautiful book is God's design for sex. Both the husband and wife pursue each other with passion. They are attracted to each other physically, but the quality of their character is what holds the relationship together. The young woman demonstrates this commitment when she tells the young man, "Place me like a seal over your heart. . . . If a man tried to buy love with all his wealth, his offer would be utterly scorned" (Song of Songs 8:6-7).

Though sex is rarely a topic that comes up in Sunday sermons or small group Bible studies, the subject should not embarrass us. God designed our bodies to find pleasure in sex. God built men and women to experience union with one another through sexual intimacy. When enjoyed properly, sex strengthens the marital relationship. When used improperly, outside of marriage, sex weakens the relationship. In any context, if sex becomes oppressive or abusive, it can leave men and women feeling callous, used, or defeated.

Song of Songs celebrates the passionate oneness that God designed for marriage. Sexuality is a gift from God to be enjoyed between a man and a woman in marriage.

God Cares about Your Emotions

We connect to God not only with our minds but also with our hearts. For example, God's assurance is based on both our knowledge and our emotions. Scripture teaches our minds to accept God's assurance, but our hearts experience this assurance through our emotions. Though our emotions are immensely important, we need more than emotions to live a life characterized by wisdom and good choices. The poetic books affirm the value of emotions but also teach us the principles we need to guide us through life. Through poetry and wisdom in Scripture, God provides answers to the questions raised by our emotions. God designed us as physical, emotional, and intellectual beings. He cares for every aspect of our being, including our emotions. The books of poetry in the Bible encourage an honest and healthy emotional connection to God. Our emotions strengthen and support our faith in God, and the five books of poetry in the Bible show us how we can glorify God through our emotions.

6

Psalms

Expressing Every Human Emotion

THE PSALMS ARE FILLED with human emotion. Each psalm is a poetic expression of feeling connected to or disconnected from the Creator. God is emotionally invested in you, and he cares about how you feel. The Psalms are the core of the Old Testament poetry books and one of the best-loved parts of Scripture. While the Psalms give voice to a wide range of human emotions, God's glory is the focus.

Though the psalms were written individually—at various times and in various settings—they were not randomly collected. The 150 psalms are arranged into five smaller books within the Hebrew Psalter, and most contemporary translations of the Bible denote the beginning of each book.

The Hebrew people set the psalms to music, and many were used originally as songs of praise in the context of communal worship. The Psalms functioned as a hymnbook for the nation of Israel. The individual psalms were written over a period of time, beginning during the early years of Israel's monarchy and continuing until the post-exilic period. After the Babylonian exile, a compiler collected and arranged all of the psalms into five books.

Authorship and Themes

Of the 150 psalms, seventy-three are attributed to David. Why did David write so many psalms? First Chronicles 15 and 16 describe his interest in creating music for public worship, and 1 Samuel 16 recounts his musical talent as he played before King Saul. David wrote many of the psalms to document and perhaps to process some of the difficult events in his life. Psalm 3 was written when he fled from his son Absalom. Psalm 51 was written after the prophet Nathan confronted him about his adultery with Bathsheba. And Psalm 57 was written when he hid from Saul in a cave. The poetic content of David's psalms aligns with events recorded in the historical books.

Other psalm writers include Solomon, Ethan, Heman, Moses, the sons of Korah, and Asaph, David's choir leader in Jerusalem. Fifty psalms have no attribution, though David may have written some of them. Some psalms have titles or notations indicating the author or setting of the psalm, or specifying musical notations, such as using a specific tune or instrument.

Each of the five books within the Psalms concludes with a doxology (a hymn of praise to God) to mark the break between them.

The Five Books	Author(s)	Doxology
Book 1: **Psalms 1–41**	Mainly David	"Praise the LORD, the God of Israel, who lives from everlasting to everlasting. Amen and amen!" (Psalm 41:13)
Book 2: **Psalms 42–72**	Mainly David and the sons of Korah	"Praise the LORD God, the God of Israel, who alone does such wonderful things. Praise his glorious name forever! Let the whole earth be filled with his glory. Amen and amen!" (Psalm 72:18-19)
Book 3: **Psalms 73–89**	Mainly Asaph	"Praise the LORD forever! Amen and amen!" (Psalm 89:52)
Book 4: **Psalms 90–106**	Mostly anonymous	"Praise the LORD, the God of Israel, who lives from everlasting to everlasting! Let all the people say, 'Amen!' Praise the LORD!" (Psalm 106:48)
Book 5: **Psalms 107–150**	Mainly David	"Let everything that breathes sing praises to the LORD! Praise the LORD!" (Psalm 150:6)

Themes are evident in each book, and the compiler of the Psalms was intentional in the order of each one. Book 1 contains many praise and worship psalms, including the beloved Psalm 23 about God's role as a shepherd to us. Book 2 includes several psalms about Israel's national interests, including God's desire to judge the wicked and deliver the righteous. Psalm 51, David's public song of repentance, is found in this book. Book 3 centers on God's sovereignty and his complete control over history. Asaph writes about God's faithfulness and his covenant in many of these psalms. Book 4 contains many anonymous psalms, covering themes of personal reflection and the limits of humanity. Book 5 contains several of David's psalms and returns to the anthems of praise found in the first book.

The five books also roughly coalesce around specific time periods. Books 1 and 2 have the early monarchy as the backdrop. Book 3 includes several laments referencing the fall of Jerusalem. Book 4 goes back to the time of Moses and serves as a reminder of Israel's identity in God. Book 5 includes psalms written after the Exile. It looks to the future and anticipates a coming king who will bring together all nations and all people.

Even though the Psalms were written by many authors over hundreds of years, a unity exists among them. God is the focus of worship in the psalms. They are honest and, at times, raw with emotion. They express the impact of pain and sin, but the thread connecting every psalm is the simple idea that God cares.

Types of Psalms

Just as there are a variety of emotions, there are a variety of psalms, each kind with its own unique tone, purpose, and content.

- *Hymns*: songs of praise and thanksgiving to God for his goodness and provision (e.g., Psalm 150)
- *Confession*: expressions of sorrow over sin (e.g., Psalm 51)
- *Wisdom*: directions for right living under God (e.g., Psalm 1)
- *Royal*: descriptions of Israel's king as God's representative (e.g., Psalm 45)
- *Imprecatory*: calls for God's judgment on enemies (e.g., Psalm 35)
- *Lament*: expressions of grief over sin that also affirm trust in God and praise God (e.g., Psalm 3)

- *Messianic*: expressions of hope and anticipation of God's anointed Messiah, Jesus Christ (e.g., Psalm 22)

Two types of psalms merit additional comment, the imprecatory psalms and the messianic psalms. The angry tone and harsh content of the imprecatory psalms can stir up controversy. However, these psalms are not about cursing enemies so much as they are a cry for God to be just. The imprecatory psalms appeal to divine justice, not human vengeance. The messianic psalms anticipate Christ's birth, his betrayal, the agony of his death on the cross, his resurrection, and even his ascension into heaven. Though these psalms were written hundreds of years before the time of Christ, their accuracy is staggering. In many ways, they function as prophecies about Jesus and his work on the cross. We can take comfort in knowing God provided a way for us to understand the events in Jesus' life through the emotions of the Psalms.

The Importance of Emotions in the Psalms

Sometimes feelings come easily. Sometimes they can be overwhelming. And then there are times when we don't know *what* we feel. In *Encountering the Book of Psalms*, Old Testament scholar C. Hassell Bullock sums up the emotional experience of the Psalms: "There is a shared humanness in the Psalter that appeals to the strongest and the weakest of us. It takes hold of us where we are, in our personal troubles and corporate crises, when our joy is inexpressible and our pain unutterable."[1]

If Psalms were only about human emotion, it would lack purpose. But because the psalms are ultimately about God, they teach us how to express our emotions in ways that glorify him. God cares deeply for us, and he is emotionally invested in us. We *feel* because we are created in God's image. With God, our emotions are purposeful, compelling us closer to him.

Psalms teaches us how to connect to God with all our emotions. And even when we don't know what we're feeling, the psalms can speak for us. As a guide for expressing our emotions in God's presence, Psalms teaches us how to grieve, rejoice, lament, confess, give thanks, and praise God. Throughout Psalms, we learn that even our most painful and difficult emotions can lead us closer to God.

7

The Major Prophets

Foretellers and Forthtellers

AFTER ISRAEL SPLIT into two kingdoms, God used a series of representatives to draw the Hebrew people and their leaders back to the covenant relationship. The prophets spoke messages of warning on God's behalf. A common mistake when reading prophetic literature in the Bible is to think of it as future predictions only. The prophets were *foretellers*, in that God gave them visions of future events. But they were primarily *forthtellers*, who issued warnings and instructions to their contemporaries on how to return to God and avoid punishment. Some prophecies predicted events far in the future, but many other prophecies were realized within a few months or years. However, more of the prophetic messages in the Old Testament warned about the consequences of sin and declared God's truth to people at the time.

The prophetic books include five major prophets followed by

twelve minor prophets. The words *major* and *minor* have nothing to do with the quality of the message or messenger. The major prophets are simply longer books, and the minor prophets are shorter books. We'll cover the major prophets in this chapter and the minor prophets in the next chapter.

Major Prophets

Isaiah	Ezekiel
Jeremiah	Daniel
Lamentations	

Minor Prophets

Hosea	Nahum
Joel	Habakkuk
Amos	Zephaniah
Obadiah	Haggai
Jonah	Zechariah
Micah	Malachi

The length of the major prophetic books can make them difficult to read in one sitting. Also, the prophecies within each book are often not in chronological order. As such, these books are among the toughest to read in the Bible.

It's important to remember that the oracles in these books were *spoken* to the people at the time, not read by them. Because a large segment of the population was illiterate, they had to *hear* God's Word in order to know it and understand it.

The Bible has two tests, or qualifications, of a prophet. First, the message must be consistent with God's previous revelation. Prophecy cannot contradict itself or lure anyone away from God. False prophets "lead you astray" and "encourage rebellion" against God (Deuteronomy 13:1-5). Second, the predictions must always come true because the words come from God. If the "prediction does not happen or come true, you will know that the LORD did not give that message" (Deuteronomy 18:21-22).

God's messengers were not hysterical or fanatical; they were humble servants. Variations of the phrase "This is what the LORD says" occur hundreds of times in the prophetic books. The prophets did not peddle their own ideas. Often at great personal expense, they spoke what God wanted the people to hear.

The prophets came from a variety of backgrounds. For example, Amos tended flocks and sycamore trees, Jeremiah was a priest, and Jonah was a well-known personality connected to people of power. How they delivered their messages also varied. Poetry, history, symbolism, and object lessons were techniques used in their prophetic presentations. The prophets were unique individuals with a variety of communication styles, but their prophetic messages all share common themes, such as God's judgment, redemption, and promises.

Prophets were necessary because the people repeatedly drifted from God. When the nation of Israel broke God's covenant relationship, he used prophets to get their attention and call them back. Israel's sins included idolatry, injustice, and traditionalism. They worshiped other gods in idolatrous acts, which is often equated to spiritual adultery. The powerful and wealthy oppressed and exploited the poor. And the formality of religion became more important than a relationship with God as the people made their worship about religious duties.

As you read through the prophets, you will once again notice a repeated cycle. The people sin, the prophet speaks a message of repentance, and God issues judgment. Yet even in this three-part cycle, God reveals the purpose of his judgment—to return the people to hope and to right relationship with him.

Isaiah: Prophet of Grace

The time of Isaiah's ministry is around 700 BC. Both the northern kingdom of Israel and the southern kingdom of Judah are in trouble and will soon go into exile. Israel is about to fall to the Assyrians (722 BC), and Judah will later fall to the Babylonians (587 BC). As an advisor in the royal court of King Hezekiah, Isaiah pleads with the people of Judah to learn from the mistakes of their kin in the northern kingdom. God promised to protect the people if they remained close to him.

Isaiah is arguably the most famous of the Old Testament prophets, and his book is often referred to as the "Gospel of the Old Testament" due to the emphasis he places on God's grace. Isaiah is quoted over sixty times in the New Testament. Strong themes of salvation are found in Isaiah. In fact, the term *salvation* appears more than twenty times in Isaiah but rarely appears in the other prophetic books.

When Isaiah wrote his book, he arranged it in two parts. As chapters were later added, a fascinating structural parallel occurred between the book of Isaiah and the Bible as a whole. Isaiah has sixty-six chapters, just as the Bible has sixty-six books. Isaiah also has two main parts, with thirty-nine chapters in the first part and twenty-seven chapters in the second part, just as the Bible has thirty-nine books in the Old Testament and twenty-seven books in the New Testament. Judgment is the prevailing theme of the first part of Isaiah, and comfort is the prevailing theme of the second part. Similarly, God's judgment in the Old Testament helps us understand God's grace in the New Testament.

Part 1: God's Judgment

The Spiritual Deterioration of Judah (Isaiah 1–12)

God's Judgment of the Corrupt Nations (Isaiah 13–27)

The Beginnings of Hope (Isaiah 28–35)

The Example of King Hezekiah (Isaiah 36–39)

Part 2: God's Comfort

The Path of Deliverance (Isaiah 40–48)

The Coming Messiah (Isaiah 49–57)

The Final Restoration (Isaiah 58–66)

The first part of Isaiah deals with the immediate threat of the Assyrians to the northern kingdom, but Isaiah also acknowledges the future threat of the Babylonians to the southern kingdom. God's people had deteriorated spiritually to the point that they were offering child sacrifices. Instead of obeying God's will, they fell into the wickedness of surrounding nations. Not only would God judge his own people, he would also judge the surrounding nations for their sins. He is just, and no one escapes his justice.

Beginning in Isaiah 40, the timeline of events jumps ahead about 150 years to the end of the Babylonian exile. The second half of the book points to God's grace and redemption. A new path of deliverance is revealed. After conquering Babylon, King Cyrus of Persia allows the exiles to return home, but the Hebrews struggle to accept God's plan. Therefore, through Isaiah, God reveals that the ultimate restoration will occur through the promised Messiah. Isaiah is a book about a stubborn people who are nevertheless loved by God. Isaiah is forthright with the people—God will judge their sin. But Isaiah also foretells the coming of a Savior who will atone for humanity's sin once and for all.

Jeremiah: The Weeping Prophet

The tone of this book is one of sadness. Jeremiah's ministry takes place between 626 and 587 BC, approximately seventy to ninety years after Isaiah's. He is often referred to as the "weeping prophet" as he is the last of God's messengers before the fall of Jerusalem. The historical setting of Jeremiah's time corresponds to the events recorded in 2 Kings 22–25.

Jeremiah communicates many of his messages through object lessons, such as cutting off his hair, not marrying, and wearing a yoke as he walked throughout the city. The purpose of these object lessons is to demonstrate the sad state of Israel in a way that is both noticeable and memorable.

Though Jeremiah was born into a family line of priests, he likely never practiced as a priest because he was called at a young age to be a prophet. He was rejected by his own people, beaten, and imprisoned. And because of the wickedness of the culture, Jeremiah was forbidden by God to marry. He often wanted to quit, and he complained to God as he struggled with his calling as a prophet.

The structure of Jeremiah begins with his calling and runs through God's judgment, ending at a point of reflection.

The Calling of Jeremiah (Jeremiah 1)

Jeremiah's Sermon before the Fall of Judah (Jeremiah 2–38)

Jerusalem Destroyed and Judah Conquered (Jeremiah 39)

Jeremiah Speaks to the Remnant of Jews (Jeremiah 40–45)

God's Judgment on Other Nations (Jeremiah 46–51)

Reflecting on Jerusalem's Destruction (Jeremiah 52)

The book contains several vivid descriptions of Judah's decline. Jeremiah uses the analogy of a failing marriage, likening Judah's pursuit of other gods to an unfaithful wife who defiles herself with other lovers. He challenges the people to remember how God previously blessed them when they were faithful. Jeremiah also compares Israel and Judah to two sisters, casting Judah as the younger sister who failed to learn from the mistakes of her unfaithful older sister, Israel. Jeremiah uses an object lesson from a potter's house. As the potter forms clay, so God shapes the nations. At the end of his message, Jeremiah smashes a jar, symbolizing Jerusalem's complete destruction.

By any worldly measure, Jeremiah was a failure. For years, he warned Judah about God's judgment, but few people listened. He faced rejection and loneliness. But Jeremiah shines as an example of one who steadfastly obeyed God's will despite terrible difficulties. In this book that bears his name, Jeremiah looks ahead and warns God's people of coming destruction. In the next book, Lamentations, Jeremiah looks back on the destruction of Jerusalem and mourns with God's people.

Lamentations: Mourning over Sin

In Lamentations, Jeremiah laments the conquest of Judah by the Babylonians. The message of the book is one of mourning over sin. As Jeremiah expresses his grief, he also affirms God's faithfulness. Even though God's people have committed egregious sins against him, God will not abandon them. As we read Lamentations, we notice three themes:

- God's people must grieve over destruction caused by sin.
- God's people must confess sin and acknowledge the righteousness of God.
- God's people can find hope in restoration.

The book is structured in a series of five poems, one per chapter.

The Desolation of Jerusalem (Lamentations 1)

The Anger of God (Lamentations 2)

The Grief of Jeremiah (Lamentations 3)

The Wrath of God (Lamentations 4)

The Prayer for Jerusalem (Lamentations 5)

The first four poems are constructed as acrostics. Lamentations 1, 2, and 4 have twenty-two verses, the first word of each verse beginning with the next acrostic letter of the Hebrew alphabet. Chapter 3 has sixty-six verses, twenty-two groups of three verses each, and the first word of each begins with the next acrostic letter. Lamentations 5 is not an acrostic, but it does contain twenty-two verses. Fortunately, the number of verses correspond to each line of poetry, which makes the poetic structure easy to follow.

As the title of the book conveys, the subject matter is grim. The text addresses such issues as famine, cannibalism, and rape. Jerusalem is a desolation, and people are starving. Jeremiah expresses deep grief over the utter ruin of Judah. God exercised his anger because the people tolerated wickedness and social injustice for too long.

Even the priests and prophets had mistreated the people for personal gain. The book ends with a prayer for Jerusalem. The people beg God to have compassion and begin the process of restoration.

Ezekiel: The Desperate Prophet

Ezekiel was written between 593 BC and 565 BC, overlapping the ministry of Jeremiah, but he speaks to Jews who were already in exile in Babylon. Unlike Jeremiah, who included many details about his life, Ezekiel doesn't reveal much about himself. Like Jeremiah, Ezekiel was born into a priestly family. He was taken captive by the Babylonians and sent into exile, where he began to prophesy.

To capture the attention of his fellow exiles, Ezekiel performs several strange prophetic acts at God's command. On a large clay brick, he draws a map of Jerusalem under siege, then places an iron griddle between himself and the brick to "demonstrate how harsh the siege will be" (Ezekiel 4:3). He lies on his left side for 390 days—and then on his right side for an additional forty days—to symbolize the years of Israel's and Judah's sins.

In one of the strangest passages in the Bible, God commands Ezekiel to cook bread over a fire of dried human dung[1] and to portion out for himself just eight ounces of bread a day for the duration of the time he will lie on his side. The dung and the small portions symbolize how Israel will eat "defiled bread in the Gentile lands" and how scarce food will be after Jerusalem falls (Ezekiel 4:13, 16). On another occasion, God commands Ezekiel to shave his head and beard with a sword. He is then to chop some of his hair, burn some, toss some to the wind, and bind some into his garment. This prophetic act foretells what will happen to the exiled citizens of Jerusalem—some would die by fire and others by the sword; some would be scattered and others saved.

The structure of Ezekiel begins with his calling and ends with a picture of the future resurrected Israel.

The Call of Ezekiel (Ezekiel 1–3)

The Judgment on Jerusalem (Ezekiel 4–24)

The Judgment on Judah's Enemies (Ezekiel 25–32)

The Resurrection of Israel (Ezekiel 33–39)

The Future of Israel (Ezekiel 40–48)

Beginning in chapter 25, the tone of the book changes from judgment of Jerusalem to judgment of Judah's enemies. These chapters look forward to the day when God will judge the nations who oppose his people. Israel's restoration begins in chapter 33 in a fascinating scene of dry bones coming to life. In chapters 40 to 48, the reference to a new Temple area is difficult to interpret. Is the passage referring to events fulfilled after the Exile or to future events not yet seen? If these events are in the future, do they refer to Israel, the church, or both? However these passages are interpreted, God's people can expect an exciting future. Ezekiel shares a glorious vision of how God will restore his people and gather them into his Kingdom.

Daniel: The Daring Prophet

Jeremiah ministered to Jews in Jerusalem. Ezekiel ministered to the Jews already in exile in Babylon. King Nebuchadnezzar rose to power in 605 BC and took Daniel and others into captivity. Daniel was about sixteen years old at the time of the Exile, and he ministered for sixty-nine years within the royal court under four Babylonian kings. Eventually, he rose to be a prime minister in Babylon. While Ezekiel preached God's truth to the Jewish people,

Daniel proclaimed God's truth within the Babylonian government. Daniel was known for his commitment to living a clean and blameless life and for the risks he took to remain true to his faith.

The writing style of Daniel differs from most other Old Testament books. It is apocalyptic in nature, like Revelation. Daniel has apocalyptic visions in which God reveals his mysteries. Daniel is a prophet during a time later described by the Gospel writer Luke as the "period of the Gentiles" (Luke 21:24). Daniel's visions reveal how the Gentiles will rule the world until the time of Christ.

The structure of Daniel is often divided into two halves.

The Events of Daniel's Life (Daniel 1–6)

Daniel's Prophetic Visions of the End of Days (Daniel 7–12)

The first six chapters of Daniel are historical and narrate the events of Daniel's life, particularly how God's sovereignty preserved Daniel and the other exiles. Narratives in Daniel 7–12 are more prophetic and record Daniel's visions of events to come. It is in this latter half of Daniel that the more apocalyptic style of writing emerges.

A key part of understanding Daniel is understanding the kings under whom he served. In Daniel 1–4, when King Nebuchadnezzar reigns, Daniel and his three compatriots—Shadrach, Meshach, and Abednego—are taken captive from Jerusalem and moved to the palace in Babylon. When Shadrach, Meshach, and Abednego refuse to bow down and worship the king's statue, they are thrown into a fiery furnace but are miraculously preserved by God.

During Belshazzar's reign (Daniel 5, 7, and 8), God reveals his judgment on the king when a mysterious disembodied hand writes an enigmatic message on a wall; the king dies that very night.

UNDERSTANDING THE BIBLE AS A WHOLE

During the reign of Darius (Daniel 6 and 9), Daniel's appointment to senior leadership over 120 of the king's other officials incurs their resentment and jealousy. They devise the wicked plot that ultimately lands Daniel in the lion's den, from which God miraculously saves him. It is then King Cyrus (Daniel 10–12), the Persian ruler who defeats the Babylonians, who issues a decree that allows the Jewish exiles to return to Jerusalem and rebuild the walls of the city. Daniel is too old to return, so Haggai, Ezra, and Nehemiah, among others, go back to start the rebuilding process.

Jesus: The Greatest Prophet

Ultimately, the Old Testament prophets point to the greatest prophet, who was yet to come. The New Testament writers refer to Jesus as a prophet, priest, and king.[2] Like the major and minor prophets, Jesus was both a foreteller and a forthteller. He issued challenges of repentance and predicted the future, including his own death and resurrection. He submitted to God's will and communicated God's message.

Christ differed from the Old Testament prophets in that he was not only a prophet, but also the fulfillment of prophecy. Many Old Testament prophecies were about Jesus. As you read through the major prophets, look for references to Christ, such as those found in Isaiah 53. That one chapter alone reveals several aspects about the crucifixion. What the Old Testament prophets proclaimed is what Christ became—the promised Messiah.

8

The Minor Prophets

Tough Reminders of God's Loving Covenant

THE NATION OF ISRAEL is in a bad spot, and the people are moving further away from God. At this stage in the Bible, readers are begging for good news. And that's the point! The Old Testament shows the problem of sin through the law, showcasing the need for the eternal solution to sin that will come through Jesus Christ.

After reading long texts of warnings by the major prophets, it is understandable why readers might want to fast-forward to the part of the story where God completes the plan of redemption. The twelve minor prophets almost feel like a broken record—repeating the same message over and over again.

When I preach from the minor prophets, I often say, "This is the part of the Bible where the pages tend to stick together," because they may not be read as often as other parts of Scripture. But if we skip these books, we will miss some amazing stories and critically important lessons from God.

In addition to their role as foretellers and forthtellers, the prophets also reminded the people about God's covenant through his law. When God gave his law to Israel in the Pentateuch, it was meant to be instructional, not merely informational. The law includes blessings for obedience and curses for disobedience. Prophetic messages serve as reminders of the consequences of not living up to the standards of the covenant. God always fulfills his obligations, and the prophets reminded the people of their own covenantal obligations.

All the prophets received a divine call and spoke God's message, not their own. As you read each book, you will notice different styles, tones, and topics. Jonah, for instance, was a grudging messenger while Habakkuk urgently pleaded with God to act. The major and minor prophets punctuate their messages with phrases such as, "This is what the Lord says," and, "[Thus] says the Lord," as reminders that God is the source. The prophets were simply messengers on God's behalf.

The Message and Messenger of Each Book

The prophets were neither radical nor innovative in the sense that they did not add their own creative touches to God's messages. Instead, they allowed God to speak through them to remind the people of their obligations under the covenant. As you read through each book, know that the overriding message is one of tough love. When they strayed, God punished the people to get their attention and draw them back to him. God's covenant was established in love, and he used strong action to remind them of his love.

Hosea

The journey through the minor prophets begins with Hosea. He lived in a time of economic prosperity in the northern kingdom of Israel. Hosea's prophesies were given right before the fall of Israel and Judah, around 722 BC. His message was a dire warning of impending collapse. Economic prosperity had brought spiritual trouble. The people had built shrines to other gods and adopted pagan practices, including prostitution, in their worship.

The subject matter and language of the book are often graphic. In one dramatic example, God tells Hosea to marry a prostitute named Gomer. The marriage symbolizes God's ongoing love and offer of grace to his people. Just as Hosea was married to an unfaithful bride, so, too, was God married to an unfaithful nation. When Gomer abandons Hosea and their children and becomes the property of another man, Hosea pursues her, buys her back, and takes her home. God longed to do the same for his people even though they were unfaithful to him.

Joel

The prophet Joel calls for religious revival because the people lack repentant hearts. The only specific event recorded in Joel is an invasion of locusts, which makes dating the book difficult. Joel mentions priests and elders but no king. Since he calls the entire nation to repentance, the omission of the king's name would be odd unless it was written after the Exile. Though the book was probably written around 500 BC, an earlier date, around the mid-800s BC, is not out of the question.

Even if the date of authorship is unclear, the message is not. God warns of judgment, and repentance is necessary to halt the coming punishment. Without humility and repentance, the people will not be able to restore their relationship with God. A day of darkness looms. Only those with right hearts will endure. Joel challenges the people, "Don't tear your clothing in your grief, but tear your hearts instead" (Joel 2:13). His point is that they need more than a superficial and outward show of repentance; they need to repent deeply and sincerely.

Amos

Amos was from the small town of Tekoa, ten miles south of Jerusalem in Judah. He was a simple shepherd who also tended a grove of sycamore trees. Traveling north to Israel, he prophesied during the time of Hosea (circa 760–750 BC). Like Hosea, Amos prophesied during a time when Israel prospered. His message is humble and transparent. Though he did not hide his lowly status as a shepherd, he was nevertheless a clever prophet.

He begins his prophetic messages by revealing God's judgment of Israel's enemies. After he has his listeners' attention, he proclaims God's judgment against Judah and Israel.

Amos reminds the people that they are not secure just because they are God's chosen people. Their security is found in God's covenant, which Israel has neglected. Though the people still perform the Temple sacrifices, it is a rote formality with no real heart behind it.

Amos preaches five visions of judgment. The images in his visions include swarms of locusts, fire, a plumb line, and a basket of summer fruit indicating that Israel is ripe for judgment. The final vision—of the Lord standing beside the altar—demonstrates that God's judgment is certain. Only those running toward God, and not away from him, will find deliverance.

Obadiah

Obadiah is the shortest book in the Old Testament, consisting of a single chapter with only twenty-one verses. Almost nothing is known about the prophet himself, but his central message is clear:

Pride is deceptive and perilous. God judges the proud and delivers the humble. The date of the book is debated. Some scholars believe it was written as early as 850 BC. Others date the book to around 586 BC, shortly after the fall of Jerusalem.

The Edomites, descendants of Esau, are the object of God's judgment. It was Esau who had sold his birthright to his younger twin brother, Jacob. The Edomites gloated over Israel's defeat rather than come to their aid. The Edomites lived in the caves among the cliffs, and their city, Petra, was perched high like an eagle's nest. The only way to approach Petra was through a long ravine. As a result, the city was well defended and hard to conquer. Obadiah writes about the impending defeat of Edom. The Edomites would eventually fade from history while Israel would rise again.

Jonah

Jonah is an example of someone with worldly success who fails spiritually. The book is unique among the Minor Prophets in that it is a personal account of a prophet at his lowest point. Jonah is neither the villain nor the hero of the narrative. The book is filled with irony, satire, and humor. Jonah was a well-known prophet of his day. He helped give King Jeroboam II of Israel the authority to extend the northern kingdom, which enabled the king to become one of the most powerful of his era.

As the book of Jonah begins, God charges the prophet to visit the Assyrian capital city of Nineveh and preach a message of repentance. As a people, the Ninevites were completely depraved—vicious enemies of Israel known for their perversion and violence. Rather than obey God's command, Jonah flees and attempts to go to Tarshish by boat rather than going to Nineveh.

To get Jonah's attention, God stirs up a storm that ultimately leads the ship's crew to throw the prophet overboard, whereupon he is promptly swallowed by a fish and remains there for three days and nights. When Jonah prays for deliverance, God rescues him by causing the fish to vomit him out.

After this remarkable ordeal, Jonah finally agrees to go to Nineveh, but only grudgingly. He preaches reluctantly, but God still uses him to bring the people of Nineveh to repentance. The book ends with Jonah stewing over God's salvation of the Ninevites. Did Jonah ever change his heart about Nineveh's salvation? The Bible doesn't say. The abrupt and incomplete ending is intended to prompt the reader to action. Jonah struggled to accept God's mission to save the lost. The implication is that God's people must step up.

Micah

Micah was a rural prophet whose message was directed to the common people. He cared deeply about how they were suffering. Like other prophets, Micah reminded the Jewish people that their persistence in sin would bring God's judgment. You can feel the tension in the book. The prophet loved his people, yet he lamented the judgments he knew were coming.

Micah lived in Moresheth, a small town about twenty-five miles south of Jerusalem in southern Judah. His prophetic message was directed against both Samaria, the capital of Israel, and Jerusalem, the capital of Judah. Micah saw the rich oppressing the poor, and he pleaded for social justice. He compared the treatment of the poor to the butchering of animals (Micah 3:1-3). The result of this depravity was the destruction of the Temple and the captivity of Jerusalem.

Micah is perhaps best known for his prophesies that foretell the future birthplace of Jesus in Bethlehem (Micah 5:2). His prophecies were so clear that Herod's scribes were able to state definitively where the Messiah would be born (Matthew 2:3-6). Another well-known statement from Micah sums up the theme of his prophetic ministry: "What does the LORD require of you? To act justly and to love mercy and to walk humbly with your God" (Micah 6:8, NIV).

Nahum

As with Jonah, Nahum prophesies the destruction of Nineveh. In Jonah, Nineveh was preserved because the people repented. However, within a few generations, the Ninevites had returned to their wickedness and God again pronounced judgment against them. In 612 BC, about fifty years after Nahum's prophecy, the Medes and Babylonians destroyed Nineveh.

As is the case with several of the minor prophets, little is known about Nahum's personal life. He prophesied sometime between 663 and 654 BC. A theme in Nahum is God's just nature. He is not morally indifferent and will deal with all sin. But Nahum also reveals the goodness of God, who is slow to anger and a stronghold for those who trust him.

Habakkuk

The book of Habakkuk, which dates to approximately 605 BC, records a fascinating conversation between the prophet and God. Habakkuk has trouble reconciling God's righteousness with the evil occurring in Judah, and he questions God about the delay in justice. Habakkuk pleads, "How long, O LORD, must I call for help? But you do not listen! 'Violence is everywhere!' I cry, but you do not come to save" (Habakkuk 1:2). God's response is unexpected. While Habakkuk decries the violence and corruption in Judah, God uses an even more wicked nation to punish the Jewish people. Habakkuk is shocked that God is going to send the Chaldeans, a group within the Babylonian empire, to conquer

Judah. In Habakkuk 2, God explains that the Chaldeans will also experience judgment after they conquer Judah. Everyone is held accountable by God's just character.

The book concludes with a song of submission. Habakkuk realizes he can see only a small part of God's sovereign plan. The prophet trusts God's wisdom and relies on him. God's glory appears, and Habakkuk sings praises.

Zephaniah

Zephaniah prophesied during the reign of King Josiah (640– 609 BC), the last good king of Judah. Zephaniah denounced the sins of Judah and the surrounding nations, but he also spoke about God's gracious response to those who demonstrate repentance.

The book begins with a warning to Judah about the coming Babylonian captivity. Every kind of idolatry is condemned, but Zephaniah also points to a time when all people will worship God, including those in "distant nations" (Zephaniah 2:11, NIV). The third and final chapter concludes by affirming God's promised restoration. God will ultimately bring everyone together, purified by him, so they can worship him and give him glory. This future time of healing and blessing will bring together not only the Jewish people but all nations.

Haggai

The final three books of the Minor Prophets, which conclude the Old Testament, are post-exilic. They were written after the Persian King Cyrus issued his decree allowing the Jewish people to return to Jerusalem following the Babylonian captivity.

Haggai lived in Babylon. When Cyrus allowed the exiles to return to Jerusalem in 538 BC, Haggai accompanied Zerubbabel, the governor, and Joshua, the high priest. Haggai was the first prophet to preach in Jerusalem following the return of the exiles. The Babylonians had destroyed Solomon's Temple in 587 BC, about sixty-six years prior.

Historically, Jerusalem embodied the national hopes of Israel, but the city was now desolate—the Temple reduced to rubble—and merely an afterthought among the nations.[1] The project of rebuilding the Temple was significant because it had long been the defining structure of Israel's identity as God's chosen people. With the Temple destroyed and God's people in exile, they had no means of engaging in communal worship, sacrifices, offerings, or festivals. In short, they had no way of formally relating to God.

The effort to rebuild Jerusalem started well, but the people became discouraged after their initial excitement. Destruction was everywhere, and everything needed attention. Sixteen years passed as the people focused on rebuilding their own homes rather than God's Temple. God expressed his disappointment with their misplaced priorities. In 520 BC, Haggai called the people back to the task of rebuilding. He, along with Zerubbabel and Joshua, led a successful project to rebuild the Temple.

Zechariah

Zechariah, a young prophet whose ministry is dated between 520 and 480 BC, stood alongside the elder Haggai as the Temple was reconstructed. Zechariah is a book of encouragement to keep the people on task with rebuilding the Temple. God would remove the mountains of difficulty before them (Zechariah 4:7).

Through a series of eight visions, Zechariah describes God's promised restoration process. The visions demonstrate how God would judge Israel's enemies, scatter their oppressors, mark off Jerusalem for protection, and remove sin. Several prophecies concerning the coming Messiah are included in this book, particularly in Zechariah 9–14. Next to Isaiah, Zechariah has more prophecies about the Messiah than any other prophetic book in the Bible.

Description of the Messiah	Zechariah's Prophecies	New Testament Fulfillment
Servant	"Soon I am going to bring my servant, the Branch" (Zechariah 3:8).	"Here is my servant whom I have chosen" (Matthew 12:18, NIV).
Branch	"Soon I am going to bring my servant, the Branch" (Zechariah 3:8). "Here is the man called the Branch. He will branch out from where he is and build the Temple of the LORD" (Zechariah 6:12).	The branch finds fulfillment in Luke 1:69-70: "He has sent us a mighty Savior from the royal line of his servant David, just as he promised through his holy prophets long ago."
King/priest	"Yes, he will build the Temple of the LORD. Then he will receive royal honor and will rule as king from his throne. He will also serve as priest from his throne, and there will be perfect harmony between his two roles" (Zechariah 6:13).	"At just the right time Christ will be revealed from heaven by the blessed and only almighty God, the King of all kings and Lord of all lords" (1 Timothy 6:15). "Jesus . . . has become our eternal High Priest in the order of Melchizedek" (Hebrews 6:20).
Humble king	"Look, your king is coming to you. He is righteous and victorious, yet he is humble, riding on a donkey—riding on a donkey's colt" (Zechariah 9:9-10).	"So they brought the colt to Jesus and threw their garments over it for him to ride on" (Luke 19:35).

Description of the Messiah	Zechariah's Prophecies	New Testament Fulfillment
Betrayed	"I said to them, 'If you like, give me my wages, whatever I am worth; butonly if you want to.' So they counted out for my wages thirty pieces of silver. And the LORD said to me, 'Throw it to the potter'—this magnificent sum at which they valued me! So I took the thirty coins and threw them to the potter in the Temple of the LORD" (Zechariah11:12-13).	"Then Judas Iscariot, one of the twelve disciples, went to the leading priests and asked, 'How much will you pay me to betray Jesus to you?' And they gave him thirty pieces of silver" (Matthew 26:14-15).
Hands pierced	"They will look on me whom they have pierced and mourn for him as for an only son. They will grieve bitterly for him as for a firstborn son who has died" (Zechariah 12:10).	"He went to the place called Place of the Skull (in Hebrew, *Golgotha*). There they nailed him to the cross" (John 19:17-18).

Malachi

In the Christian canon, Malachi is the final book of the Old Testament. The prophet lived in Judah following the return to Jerusalem, and his prophetic message is dated to about 430 BC. The book is a rebuke against the Jewish people and their disregard for genuine worship. It was written about a hundred years after the Jews had returned to Jerusalem from exile, and serves as a bridge between the Old Testament and the New Testament.

Malachi addresses the sins of the priests, who were irreverent and neglectful. They were refusing to work unless paid for their duties.

The people had become spiritually lax and did not fear God, even to the point of cheating him of tithes and offerings (Malachi 3:8). The final sentence in Malachi is a warning from God: "Otherwise I will come and strike the land with a curse" (Malachi 4:6), which leaves the term *curse* as the last word in the Old Testament. In a prophetic reference to John the Baptist, Malachi looks forward by announcing God's promise to send another messenger to "prepare the way before me" (Malachi 3:1). God's messenger would reveal God's plan for redeeming his people.

The Blank Page and Four Hundred Years of Silence

As the Old Testament transitions to the New Testament, God goes silent. In many Bibles, a page is intentionally left blank between the two Testaments to represent the four hundred years in which God did not speak. Even in his silence, however, he was working. During this time, the Hebrew people lived under several political powers. Portions of Daniel's prophecy come true as power transfers from one nation to the next.

Persian rule 539–331 BC

Greek rule 331–167 BC

Egyptian rule (Ptolemy) 320–198 BC

Syrian rule 198–167 BC

Jewish self-rule (Maccabean and Hasmonean periods) 167–63 BC

Roman rule 63 BC–AD 70

Segments of the Dead Sea Scrolls, ancient Hebrew manuscripts found in the Qumran caves in the Judaean Desert, were written during the intertestamental period. A collection of historical works, subsequently referred to as the Apocrypha, were also written. These books were written in Greek and provide much of the historical background of Jewish life two centuries prior to Jesus Christ. Though the apocryphal books are not accepted as Scripture by Protestants, they do provide helpful information and insights for understanding the context of Jewish life at the time.

The Septuagint, a Greek translation of the Old Testament, was also written during this four-hundred-year time period. Many Jews remained dispersed outside of the nations of Israel and Judah and lost the ability to speak Hebrew. When Greek become the dominant world language, the Old Testament was translated into Greek. This translation become known as the Septuagint, often abbreviated as LXX (or seventy) because of the seventy scholars who helped translate it.

Several groups also began to form during the intertestamental period. Pharisees, Sadducees, and institutions such as the synagogue and the Sanhedrin took shape and rose to power. The Pharisees guarded the observance of the law in a way that was similar to how the prophets had reminded the Hebrew people about their obligations to God's covenant. The synagogue became a place for exiles to worship while they were away from the Jerusalem Temple. The Sadducees were a political force in Israel, and they aligned with the occupying and civil power structures of the time. While the Pharisees were religious and held to conservative views of the Old Testament, the Sadducees were political and held to liberal views, even denying the resurrection from the dead. The Sanhedrin was the highest religious governing body. It was made up of the high priest, twenty-four chief priests, twenty-four elders, and twenty-two scribes. They existed to protect the Jewish way of life. By the time of Christ, they had become an oppressive power structure, lording their authority over the people.

After four hundred years, many people had given up hope that the Messiah would ever come. Still, some remained faithful, while others practiced the forms of religion but without giving God their hearts. God's next prophet, John the Baptist, came with a clear message: "Repent of your sins and turn to God, for the Kingdom of Heaven is near" (Matthew 3:2). After four centuries of silence, God was speaking again, and everyone expected the Messiah to come soon (Luke 3:15). A new covenant would reveal God's plan for saving not only Israel, but the entire world.

PART II

THE NEW TESTAMENT

9

The Gospels and Acts

Good News Arrives

GOD INITIATED A NEW covenant, but a clear connection exists between the Old Testament and the New Testament. With the coming of Jesus, the law was fulfilled, not invalidated. The people of Israel had wrongly interpreted their chosen status as "a matter of position and privilege rather than a matter of purpose and call."[1] The Jewish people were not chosen because God loved them more or because they were more special than others. They were chosen because they were called to be the conduit of grace, the channel by which God's Good News would go to every tongue, tribe, and nation. However, when Jesus arrived, the Jewish people were expecting a savior of Israel, not a Savior of the world.

The first book of the New Testament, Matthew begins with a genealogy of Jesus, which serves as a bridge between the Old Testament and the New Testament. Jesus' genealogy connects him to the covenants in the Old Testament. Jesus is the Son of God but also the son of David and the son of Abraham. The New Testament is not a new story but a continuation of the story God began in Genesis. Jesus is the fulfillment of the promises God made to Abraham and David.

After four hundred years with no prophetic voice in Israel, the Good News finally arrives. It is often referred to as the *gospel*, from the Greek word *euangelion*, which means "good news."[2] The Good News is not only the message about Jesus. The Good News *is* Jesus. As pastor Tim Keller puts it, "The gospel is not the first step in a stairway of truths; rather, it is more like the hub in a wheel of truth."[3] Jesus doesn't just save us in a moment in time; our salvation stays with us for eternity. Jesus is more than the messenger or carrier of the gospel, and the gospel is more than just the history of salvation. Jesus *is* the gospel, and the gospel informs every aspect of our lives.

At first glance, it might seem that the four Gospels—Matthew, Mark, Luke, and John—were placed first in the New Testament because they were written first, but that is not necessarily true. The good news about Jesus was first communicated by word of mouth. Then apostles of Jesus (primarily Paul) wrote letters (also called *epistles*) to believers in various locations in southern Europe and Asia Minor, many of which predate the writing of the four Gospels. Matthew, Mark, Luke, and John penned their Gospels to tell the story of Jesus that people throughout the Near East were already hearing and reading.

Matthew, Mark, and Luke share a lot of the same content and are often called the *synoptic* Gospels, reflecting the common viewpoint of their stories, whereas John's Gospel tells the story of Jesus' ministry more through theological discourses. Each Gospel also has a separate audience. Matthew wrote to a Jewish audience and focuses on Jesus as king. Many Old Testament fulfillment passages appear in Matthew because of his focus on showing Jesus as the Son of David. Mark, writing to Gentile Christians in Rome, records a rapid-fire narrative of Jesus' miracles. The Romans were action-oriented and wanted to know what Jesus had done, not necessarily what prophecies he had fulfilled. Luke had a Greek audience and connected Jesus to Adam because of the interests his audience had in humanity and ideals. John wrote to demonstrate that salvation is available to everyone.

The following chart provides a brief overview of each Gospel.

Gospel Writer	Audience	Style	How Christ Is Presented	How to Read
Matthew, one of the original twelve disciples	Jews	Jesus' teaching presented in long blocks	The King (Matthew 2:1-12)	Jesus fulfills Old Testament prophecies
Mark, a disciple of Jesus and an assistant to Peter	Gentile Christians in Rome	Fast-moving; focused on events and what Jesus did	The Suffering Servant (Mark 10:35-45)	Jesus performs miracles to prove his divinity
Luke, a Gentile doctor and a traveling companion of Paul	Greeks	Detailed collection of others' stories	The Son of Man (Luke 4:1-13)	Jesus cares for everyone, including outcasts
John, one of the original twelve disciples	Gentile Christians	Reflective and explanatory teaching	The Son of God (John 1:1-18)	Jesus wants you to know he is God

Throughout his ministry, Jesus told people he must go to Jerusalem, which is where his purpose would be fulfilled. Jesus went to Jerusalem to complete God's plan of redemption. He atoned for our sins on the cross and rose again to provide eternal life. The Gospels record his ministry, culminating in his movement toward the city.

The church formed shortly after Christ's ascension, but the church was not to stay only in Jerusalem. Instead, they were to move outward to share the good news about Jesus with the world. The book of Acts records the early church's movement away from Jerusalem.

What began in the book of Acts continues today. The mission of sharing Jesus has not changed, and every church today has the responsibility to continue the work of evangelism and discipleship. The book of Acts is both a historical narrative of the early church and an inspiring message for churches today.

Matthew: Jesus Is the Messiah for the Jews

Matthew was a tax collector and thus was despised by the common people. Those who wanted to be tax collectors made a bid to the Roman government for the job, then used their power to extort and overtax people for their own gain. At times, the monies they collected were used to fund Roman military efforts to subjugate people in the empire, including the Jewish people. When Jesus approached, Matthew was sitting at a tax collector's booth. Jesus challenged Matthew to leave everything and follow him, which is exactly what Matthew did.

At the time that Matthew wrote his Gospel, Israel was still under Roman rule. However, the language Matthew uses is not Latin but Greek, which was the preferred language of written communication at the time. The Good News is spreading beyond

Jerusalem as persecution against Jewish Christians has prompted many to flee. Matthew presents Jesus as a King ushering in an eternal Kingdom. Jesus is the long-anticipated Messiah, the one God covenanted to send from the beginning of the Bible.

The first sentence of Matthew is a direct tie to the Old Testament. There are two key covenants from God concerning the Jewish people, and Matthew connects Jesus to both. Jesus is the "Son of David" and the "Son of Abraham" (Matthew 1:1, NKJV). Through David, God promised Israel a king to sit on the throne forever (2 Samuel 7:8-13). Through Abraham, God promised to bless all the families on earth (Genesis 12:3). David's descendant would rule. Abraham's descendant would be sacrificed. Matthew's Gospel opens with the birth of a king and concludes with the offering of a sacrifice.

Matthew's audience is primarily the Jewish people, though it is not restricted to them. He includes dozens of quotes from the Old Testament and references how Jesus fulfilled the prophetic works. Matthew makes frequent use of Jewish terminology and also assumes the reader understands Jewish customs.

The structure of Matthew is tied to both geography and five discourses. At the beginning of chapter 19, Jesus crosses the Jordan River, ending his Galilean ministry and entering Judea on his way to Jerusalem.

Introduction of the Messiah: Jesus' birth, baptism, and temptation (Matthew 1:1–4:11)

The Messiah Ministers in Galilee (Matthew 4:12–18:35)
    Jesus Teaches (Matthew 5–7)
    Jesus Serves (Matthew 8–10)
    People React (Matthew 11–18)

The Messiah Ministers in Judea (Matthew 19–28)
    Jesus as King (Matthew 19–25)
    Jesus Crucified (Matthew 26–27)
    Jesus Resurrected (Matthew 28)

The five discourses in Matthew's narrative are each marked by the phrase "when Jesus had finished saying these things" or something similar (see Matthew 7:28; 11:1; 13:53; 19:1; 26:1). These blocks of Jesus' teaching are important components within Matthew, demonstrating Jesus understood his role as the Messiah.

Sermon on the Mount	Matthew 5–7	Jesus shares what establishes God's Kingdom
Instructing the Twelve Disciples	Matthew 10	Followers of Jesus are to spread the gospel
Kingdom Parables (Part 1)	Matthew 13	The Kingdom will grow despite persecution
Kingdom Parables (Part 2)	Matthew 18	How disciples are to relate to each other
The Olivet Discourse	Matthew 24–25	Prophetic events leading to the Second Coming

The conclusion of Matthew reveals the coming mission of the church. Following his resurrection, Jesus meets the eleven remaining disciples (minus Judas) at a mountain in Galilee. They had experienced many highs and lows together. Now Jesus gathers them for his last words before he ascends into heaven (Matthew 28:16-20). He makes a great claim that he has all authority. He issues a great commission to go to all nations and make disciples. And he makes a great promise that he will be with them always. In Matthew 24:14, Jesus had told them the Good News would go to the entire world, and then the end would come. As Jesus gives them the Great Commission in Matthew 28, he reveals that they will be the ones to make disciples of all nations.

Jesus' Great Commission to the disciples is for us just as much as it was for them. We learn about our calling as well. The gospel will get to all peoples. It will go to every nation and tribe. If you care about the end of the story, then you will work to complete the story. You are God's promise to the nations.

Mark: Jesus Is the Suffering Servant for the Romans

The shortest of the four Gospels, Mark is often underrated and neglected. Mark is also the earliest of the four Gospels, containing less teaching and more narrative about Jesus' miracles and his ministry. The style of the book is straightforward and rapid-fire. Mark uses words such as *immediately* and *then* to make quick transitions in the flow of the story. These transitions demonstrate the urgency of the gospel. Mark pushes the reader through the story quickly to elicit a response to the gospel.

Mark was a companion of Paul and Barnabas and was mentored by Peter. He is sometimes referred to as John Mark, as John was his Jewish name and Mark was his Roman name. Peter references Mark as "my son" in his first letter (1 Peter 5:13). Given the prominence of Peter in Mark's Gospel, it is likely that Mark recorded many of Peter's eyewitness accounts in the narrative. Unlike Matthew, Mark does not try to prove fulfillment of the Old Testament prophecies. The reason is his audience. Mark is writing to the Romans, who are a "show me" people. They had little connection to Jewish history, but they were interested in Jesus' work.

Mark records only four parables but includes several of Jesus' miracles. He does not include an account of Jesus' birth, nor of Jesus' teaching in the Sermon on the Mount. Why? Because Mark portrays Jesus more as a working servant and less as a Jewish king. Jesus came to touch lepers, heal the masses, feed thousands, care for prostitutes, and wash dirty feet. Because God himself serves, the heavenly standard for greatness is servanthood (Mark 10:45). Jesus' work on the cross is what atones for sin, and only he can pay our debt.

Mark's Gospel appeared as members of the early church were being executed under the tyranny of Nero, the Roman emperor. Some believers were being mauled by lions or burned alive, and both Peter and Paul died as martyrs—Peter by crucifixion and Paul likely by beheading. Mark sought to reassure the early believers by reminding them of Jesus' own suffering and that they were partaking in his suffering for the cause of Christ. Not only were the Romans interested in Christ's work, they were also drawn to the themes of suffering reflected in Mark's Gospel.

After beginning with the announcement of Good News, the structure of Mark's Gospel reveals how Jesus serves people, sacrifices for them, and ultimately saves them through his resurrection.

Announcing the Good News of Jesus (Mark 1:1-13)

Jesus Serves People (Mark 1:14–8:30)

Jesus Sacrifices for the World (Mark 8:31–15:47)

The Resurrection of Jesus (Mark 16:1-20)

The turning point in Mark comes in chapter 8. After healing a blind man, Jesus goes with the disciples to the villages around Caesarea Philippi, near the foot of Mount Hermon. Jesus is within a few short months of his arrest and crucifixion. Now is the time for him to reveal his identity to his disciples. He poses the most important question in all of eternity: "Who do you say I am?" Peter recognizes Jesus as Lord and responds, "You are the Messiah" (Mark 8:29).

Following Peter's confession, Jesus predicts his coming suffering, including his death on the cross. The tone of Mark's writing changes following this account. Jesus moves from a place of *service* to one of *sacrifice*. There is no clearer picture of Jesus as a Suffering Servant than the one presented in Mark.

The last chapter of Mark includes a section of debated text. Mark 16:9-20 is often set in brackets in English translations of the Bible because there is disagreement among scholars about whether it was part of Mark's original Gospel. Below is a brief summary of arguments on both sides of the debate. Personally, I lean toward including the text in the canon of Scripture. Whichever side you take in this debate, the inclusion or exclusion of the text does not change the meaning of Scripture.

Mark 16:9-20 Is Original to Scripture	Mark 16:9-20 Is Not Original to Scripture
Most of Mark is Peter's recollections written down by Mark. Mark himself added Mark 16:9-20 to include the Resurrection.	The style and grammar of Mark 16:9-20 do not match the rest of Mark. Several words and expressions are different in the ending.
Why would a Gospel writer exclude the Resurrection? Abrupt or suspended endings were rare as a literary device during this time.	Mark intentionally left readers hanging, wanting more. If an abrupt or suspended ending were to occur, then this is where it would occur.
Ninety-five percent of the original manuscripts include Mark 16:9-20.	The two oldest existing manuscripts, Codex Vaticanus and Codex Sinaiticus, do not include the longer ending.
Early church fathers Irenaeus and Justin Martyr claim the longer ending.	Other church fathers, such as Jerome and Eusebius, question the authenticity of the longer ending.

Luke: Jesus Is Hope for the Gentiles

If Mark is known for writing with brevity and a sense of urgency, then Luke is known for being a careful collector of details. Luke's Gospel is the longest book in the New Testament and was written to be a companion work to the book of Acts. Luke wrote both books, and together they cover about sixty-five years of history. Combined, Luke and Acts make up over a quarter of the New Testament. The apostle Paul wrote more books than any other New Testament writer, but Luke wrote more text. The Gospel of Luke contains the most thorough account of God's plan of redemption. The theme of salvation stands out.

Despite the extensiveness of both Luke and Acts, we know less about Luke as a person than any other New Testament author. He rarely refers to himself in either book. As an educated physician, Luke is among the first scholars to investigate the claims of Christ. He is most likely a Gentile, the only one to write a New Testament book, and he also served as a traveling companion and friend to Paul. Luke wrote in elegant Greek to a predominantly Greek audience. He was not an eyewitness, but he carefully examined the reports of others, especially those of Peter and the women who followed Christ (Luke 5:3; 8:2-3).

The first four verses of this Gospel are a grand opening to a detailed work. Luke had investigated the claims of eyewitnesses, and those who told the story of Jesus are validated by Luke's careful examination. Writing to a person of importance, the most honorable Theophilus, Luke preserves the numerous accounts of Jesus and his ministry. Theophilus was probably an influential leader among the Christians in Greece, perhaps helping to fund missionary endeavors. The audience of this Gospel also includes other Gentiles. The Greeks valued beauty, rhetoric, and philosophy, which made them a very different audience than the Romans to whom Mark wrote. With their broad cultural influence, the Greeks would have been drawn in by the writing of Luke, an educated Greek doctor. He was the perfect person to write to them about Jesus' humanity.

Luke is writing at a time when Christians were distancing their practices from Judaism, and he clearly states his purpose from the beginning: "So you can be certain of the truth of everything you were taught" (Luke 1:4). As a Gentile himself, Luke wants his Gentile readers to have assurance of their faith.

One way to view the structure of Luke's Gospel is through geography. After the birth narrative, Luke tracks Jesus' ministry from Galilee into Jerusalem and to the cross.

Jesus' Birth and Development (Luke 1:1–4:13)

Jesus' Ministry in Galilee (Luke 4:14–9:50)

Jesus' Journey to Jerusalem (Luke 9:51–19:44)

Jesus' Sacrifice and Triumph over Death (Luke 19:45–24:53)

Though Matthew, Mark, and Luke share a lot of content and record the same stories, several themes distinguish Luke from the other Gospels. Prayer is prominent as a spiritual discipline. Jesus both depended on prayer and taught much about prayer. The Holy Spirit plays a more prominent role in Luke's Gospel, including Jesus' conception. Women are also prominently featured in this book. Luke alone records the following:

Elizabeth's Miraculous Pregnancy with John the Baptist (Luke 1)

Anna's Adoration of Jesus (Luke 2:36-38)

Jesus Forgiving the Prostitute (Luke 7:37-50)

Jesus Healing the Woman Who Had Been Afflicted by an
Evil Spirit for Eighteen Years (Luke 13:10-17)

The genealogy accounts in Matthew and Luke also contain different perspectives. While Matthew focuses on establishing Jesus'
connection to the Davidic throne and therefore traces his genealogy through Joseph starting with Abraham, Luke focuses on Jesus'
humanity and therefore traces his genealogy through Mary, going
all the way back to Adam.

Luke demonstrates his focus on Jesus' humanity when he gives
us the particulars of Jesus' birth. He writes about how the creator
of the universe entered the world like everyone else and had to
grow in wisdom and stature. Someone had to change God's dirty
diapers. As a child, the omnipotent Savior learned to walk. As a
young man, the omniscient Messiah learned the trade of a carpenter. Luke's focus on the humanity of Jesus reminds us how God
relates to his creation.

Luke also focuses on themes of compassion—how Jesus works
on behalf of sinners and outcasts. Luke clearly portrays Jesus as
God incarnate. He reveals a Savior with sympathies, feelings, and
emotions—the glory of God descended to our level. Parables such as
the Good Samaritan and the Prodigal Son serve as reminders of God's
desire to save all people. God wants a relationship with his creation,
and Luke tells a powerful story of the Good News available to all.

John: Jesus Is the Savior of the World

John wrote his Gospel about fifty years after the end of Jesus'
earthly ministry. Christianity was spreading rapidly, and persecution from the Roman government was becoming more common.
Now in his later years, John writes to supplement the other three
Gospels. He focuses on Jesus' deity and how Jesus, who is God,

became human. John describes from a theological perspective how Jesus is both fully human *and* fully divine.

John is writing after the fall of Jerusalem (which happened in AD 70), and he omits several items included in the other Gospels. There are no genealogies, no birth account, nothing about Jesus' boyhood, no temptation narrative, no account of the Transfiguration, no account of the Ascension, and no mention of the Great Commission. John assumes his readers understand Jesus' story from the other three Gospels. But because false teaching about Jesus—denying Jesus as the Son of God—is circulating, John's Gospel makes it a point to elevate and exalt Christ as God and emphasize Jesus' deity throughout.

Jesus as Portrayed in the Synoptic Gospels	Jesus as Portrayed in John's Gospel
Narrative of Jesus' ministry	Theology of Jesus' identity
Jesus outwardly	Jesus inwardly
Humanity of Jesus	Divinity of Jesus
Public ministry of Jesus	Private conversations and thoughts of Jesus

Like his brother James, John was a fisherman, and the two were referred to as the "Sons of Thunder" (Mark 3:17). Along with James and Peter, John was especially close to Jesus. In his Gospel, rather than mentioning his own name, he humbly refers to himself as "the one whom Jesus loved" (John 20:2). He also wrote three letters (1, 2, and 3 John) and the book of Revelation.

John had first been a follower of John the Baptist, and later in life he was the pastor of the church in Ephesus. Eventually he was banished to the island of Patmos, where he wrote Revelation.

John was Jesus' youngest disciple and also lived to be the oldest—probably into his nineties. A prominent theme of John's

Gospel is the call to *believe*, a word that appears almost a hundred times in John.

After introducing Jesus as the Word made flesh, John's Gospel moves from Jesus' public ministry to his private ministry among his disciples. The book ends with Jesus' trial, crucifixion, and resurrection.

Jesus the Word Incarnate (John 1:1-18)

The Public Ministry of Jesus—Miracles and Conversations (John 1:19–12:50)

The Private Ministry of Jesus—Teaching and Training Disciples (John 13:1–17:26)

Jesus Arrested, Tried, and Crucified (John 18:1–19:42)

Jesus Resurrected and Alive (John 20:1–21:25)

Another unique aspect of John is the use of the number seven, often symbolizing completion or fullness. There are seven miracles or signs pointing to the divinity of Jesus. And there are seven "I am" statements Jesus makes of himself to reveal his deity. As you read through John, take note of the use of these groups of seven.

Seven Signs Proving Jesus Is God

Turns water into wine (John 2:1-11)

Heals the nobleman's son (John 4:46-54)

Heals the man at Bethesda (John 5:1-47)

Feeds the 5,000 (John 6:1-14)

Walks on water (John 6:16-21)

Heals the blind man (John 9:1-41)

Raises Lazarus from the dead (John 11:1-57)

Seven "I Am" Statements Revealing Jesus Is God

"I am the bread of life" (John 6:35, 48, 51)

"I am the light of the world" (John 8:12; 9:5)

"I am the gate" (John 10:7, 9)

"I am the good shepherd" (John 10:11, 14)

"I am the resurrection and the life" (John 11:25)

"I am the way, the truth, and the life" (John 14:6)

"I am the true vine" (John 15:1, NIV)

All four Gospels answer the question, Who is Jesus? Matthew focuses on Jesus as king for a Jewish audience. Mark records many miracles to prove to the Gentiles in Rome that Jesus is God. Luke reveals the humanity of Jesus for a Greek audience. John's Gospel is about Jesus' divinity. The prologue in John 1 shows that Jesus was present with God from the beginning. While Matthew begins with the genealogy of Jesus, Mark begins with the testimony of John the Baptist, and Luke begins with the birth narrative, John begins where Genesis 1 begins—when there was nothing but God. According to John and his reference to Jesus as "the Word," Jesus *is* the beginning, which makes him God.

Acts: The Church Begins in Jerusalem

While Luke's Gospel shows Jesus' movement *toward* Jerusalem, Acts records the church's movement *away* from Jerusalem. While the Gospel of Luke is the story of Christ's *coming*, Acts is the story of the church *going*. Acts is a historical link between the Gospels and the letters (epistles) that make up the remainder of the New Testament. Though sometimes called the Acts of the Apostles, the book is not so much a record of what the apostles did as it is a record of what the Holy Spirit did. Without Acts, we would know nothing of Pentecost (the descent of the Holy Spirit on Jesus' followers), the martyrdom of Stephen, or how the gospel message extended beyond Jerusalem to reach the Gentiles.

Both Luke and Acts are written to Theophilus, as indicated in the introductions of both books. Consider Luke's Gospel as part one of the story and the book of Acts as part two of the story. Luke was not an eyewitness to the events in his Gospel, and so he relied on the accounts of others. However, Luke *was* an eyewitness to the events recorded in Acts, especially in the second half. Luke's Gospel is more about what Christ did on earth, while Acts is more about what God continued to do through the Holy Spirit.

The Gospels	The Book of Acts
The power of the Resurrection	The power of the Holy Spirit
The mission Christ began	The mission we are to complete
Jesus crucified and resurrected	Jesus ascended and exalted
Christ's teachings	The effects of Christ's teachings

The book of Acts can be divided into two halves.

Repentance (Acts 1–12)

Belief (Acts 13–28)

In the first half, Peter is leading a group to witness primarily to the Jewish people. Repentance stands out as a theme. In the second half of Acts, Paul is witnessing primarily to the Gentiles. Belief stands out as the theme. The book of Acts solidifies the purpose of the church, which is to be the vehicle by which the gospel goes to others.

Part 1 (Acts 1–12)	Part 2 (Acts 13–28)
Jerusalem is the center	Antioch is the center
Peter is the main leader	Paul is the main leader
The gospel is preached to Jerusalem, Judea, and Samaria	The gospel is preached to the ends of the earth
Peter is imprisoned	Paul is imprisoned

As the book begins, the apostles return to Jerusalem after Jesus ascends into heaven. They go to an "upper room," likely a rooftop of a home reached by outside stairs. Women join them—other followers and likely their wives as well. What is the first recorded activity of the early Christian community? Prayer. They were waiting. Jesus promised something big—a movement. So they prayed.

Imagine the emotions of those in the upper room. Some had witnessed the brutality of Jesus' crucifixion. All had experienced the confusion of an empty tomb, and then the wonder—and doubt—of a resurrected Jesus. After the surprise of his miraculous resurrection settles, Jesus unexpectedly ascends to heaven. What is next? They have jobs. They have families.

The Day of Pentecost arrives, along with an unmistakable sign of God's power in their lives. A group of 120 who had gathered in the upper room rush out into the Temple courts, where more than 3,000 people are milling about. These uneducated Galileans start speaking in different languages, and the people are astounded and perplexed. The list of nations in Acts 2 echoes the table of nations in Genesis 10. The attempt to build a tower to God in Genesis 11 resulted in the confusion of everyone's language. Now in Acts, the curse of Babel is reversed as the gospel is shared in ways people from every nation can understand. From this point forward in the book of Acts, God makes clear his desire for the Good News to go from Jerusalem to the ends of the earth.

Sharing the Good News of Jesus

The four Gospels are books *about* Jesus; they were not written *by* Jesus. Matthew, Mark, Luke, and John record Jesus' teaching, his words, and the narratives surrounding his ministry. The fact that Jesus did not write his own Gospel should not disturb us. Rather, the four Gospels show the strength of God's revelation through the inspiration of the Holy Spirit. With the accounts of Matthew, Mark, Luke, and John, we not only have what Jesus said, but also what he did from the perspective of those whom he redeemed.

Acts continues the story of Jesus through the mission of the local church. The Good News begins in Jerusalem and spreads to Judea and Samaria next. By Acts 10, Gentiles are accepting the gospel, surprising Jewish converts in Jerusalem. God reveals his message is for everyone. In Acts 12, the gospel goes to Asia, then to what is modern Europe in Acts 16. The story ends with the Good News arriving in Rome. Along the way, the church suffers persecution, and key leaders are martyred. But nothing stops God's mission to seek and to save the lost. Jesus promised that the powers of hell could not conquer the church (Matthew 16:18). The book of Acts tells the story of hell defeated and heaven prevailing.

10

Paul's Letters to Churches

Encouragement, Correction, and Direction

FROM THE DARKNESS of prison, the apostle Paul wrote incredible words of encouragement to the Philippian church. The deep connection of trust and love between Paul and the Philippians is evident in his letter. Even though he was in prison, Paul wrote that his predicament had "helped to spread the Good News" and that the Philippians should "rejoice" with him (Philippians 1:12; 4:4). Paul's letter to the Philippians is a high-water mark of encouragement, but his letters to other churches included rebukes and corrections. Writing letters had not been a typical method of religious instruction among the Jewish people, but it became a preferred form of communication to disseminate information relatively quickly among a growing body of people spread out over a large geographic area.[1]

The apostle Paul is responsible for writing thirteen of the twenty-seven books in the New Testament. All his works are letters written to churches or individuals between AD 50 and 70. We'll cover Paul's letters written to churches in this chapter and those written to individuals in the next two chapters.

Letters to Churches

Romans	Philippians
1 and 2 Corinthians	Colossians
Galatians	1 and 2 Thessalonians
Ephesians	

Letters to Individuals

1 and 2 Timothy	Philemon
Titus	

The apostle Paul's given name was Saul. He was born in the city of Tarsus, in what is modern-day Turkey. His parents were Pharisees and raised him as a religious Jewish nationalist. As a young man, Saul learned under the great rabbi Gamaliel and became a religious extremist, highly educated in the Jewish Scriptures. Saul spent his early career persecuting Christians, to the point that he sought to "destroy the church" by imprisoning both Christian men and women (Acts 8:3).

The pivotal moment in Saul's life occurred on the Damascus Road, when Jesus spoke to him through a bright light. Temporarily blinded, Saul was led to a Christian named Ananias, who helped him realize the truth of Christ. The persecutor of the early church would soon become a missionary for the expansion of God's Kingdom. His name was changed to Paul, but more importantly, his zealousness was now for Christ alone.

Before embarking on his missionary journeys, Paul spent three years in Arabia preparing. His combination of Roman citizenship, Greek education, and Hebrew religion helped equip him for the task of expanding the early church. Over the course of three missionary journeys and his final journey to Rome, Paul planted churches, wrote letters, and encouraged young churches to hold to God's truth and share the Good News about Jesus. Even as he experienced persecution and imprisonment, Paul never lost sight of God's mission to reach not only Jewish people but also Gentiles.

As you read Paul's letters, note the differences in subject matter and tone. The Philippian church was in great shape, so Paul wrote to encourage them. The Corinthian church had many problems, and Paul wrote to correct them. The Galatian church was suffering doctrinal attacks from a legalistic, religious sect of Judaizers, while the Colossian church was influenced by the philosophy of Gnosticism. Every letter was written to address a specific circumstance. That means his letters are "occasional" in nature, written in response to a problem or situation within the church. Paul wrote *to* a particular people *in* a particular place and time. To understand Paul's teaching, it is wise to learn as much as possible about the context within which the letters were written. The letters should also be read in their entirety to avoid taking individual passages out of context.

We begin with a letter that helped develop the doctrine of the church. Romans is the longest letter and arguably the deepest theologically.

Romans: Developing Doctrine and Applying Doctrine

The placement of Romans after Acts is no accident. Luke wrote Acts to provide a historical narrative about the growth of the early church. And Paul wrote Romans (circa AD 56–58) to help develop the doctrine of the church. With these two books, we begin to understand how the church expanded outward on mission as it deepened roots theologically.

The first chapter of Romans gives a dismal picture of the human condition—the downward spiral of sin leads everyone to death. But there is also good news—anyone can be made righteous through the power of Christ's salvation. The structure of Romans falls into two parts:

Theology and Doctrine (Romans 1–8)

Life Application (Romans 9–16)

In Romans 1–8, Paul masterfully reveals the proper theology and doctrine of the church. In Romans 9–16, he gives the life application of these doctrines. The first half of the book develops what the church believes, and the second half of the book details how we should live what we believe.

The gospel of salvation is at the center of Romans. In the first four chapters, Paul explains why it is necessary for God to show his righteousness and why people can experience this righteousness only by faith alone. In Romans 5–8, Paul discusses the significance of justification—that sin no longer has a hold on us and the law no longer controls us. It is through the Holy Spirit that the Christian enjoys the assurance of eternal victory. In Romans 9–11, Paul focuses on Israel. He explains that not all Hebrew people will accept God's salvation, but through Israel, God brought salvation to anyone who accepts Christ. In Romans 12–16, Paul examines the more practical question of what it looks like to live as grace-filled, gospel-focused people.

Common throughout the book is the linguistic device called a *diatribe*, in which a teacher persuades students using a back-and-forth dialogue with rhetorical questions and answers. This ancient form of argumentation was popular at the time and is prominent in Romans 6–7.

Passage	Rhetorical Question	Answer
Romans 6:1-2	"Well then, should we keep on sinning so that God can show us more and more of his wonderful grace?"	"Of course not! Since we have died to sin, how can we continue to live in it?"
Romans 6:15-16	"Well then, since God's grace has set us free from the law, does that mean we can go on sinning?"	"Of course not! Don't you realize that you become the slave of whatever you choose to obey?"
Romans 7:7	"Well then, am I suggesting that the law of God is sinful?"	"Of course not! In fact, it was the law that showed me my sin."
Romans 7:13	"But how can that be? Did the law, which is good, cause my death?"	"Of course not! Sin used what was good to bring about my condemnation to death. So we can see how terrible sin really is."

Some of the most prominent Christian leaders in history accepted Christ as a result of reading Romans. Sixteenth-century church reformer Martin Luther studied Romans and called it the "very purest gospel" and the "chief part of the New Testament."[2]

In Romans, Paul details how we are sinful by nature and how Christ saves us. Several key doctrines of the faith are rooted in this letter:

- *regeneration*: God's work to give us new spiritual life
- *conversion*: our willing response to the good news of Jesus
- *justification*: God declares us righteous, having right legal standing before God
- *adoption*: an act of God to bring us into his family
- *sanctification*: the progressive work of the Holy Spirit in our lives to make us more like Christ

Romans is a rich book, filled with theology and life application. At times, the letter is not an easy read, but it is supremely edifying.

1 and 2 Corinthians: Correcting Error in the Church

Not every New Testament church is worth emulating. The Corinthian church struggled, and Paul wrote two letters correcting errors in their congregation. Acts 18 tells us that Paul went to Corinth to share the gospel. He looked for work and found it in the shop of Priscilla and Aquila. He then began to preach in the synagogues.

Paul wrote 1 Corinthians in response to a previous letter he had received from the church (mentioned in 1 Corinthians 7:1). While Paul was in Ephesus on his third missionary journey, he received a report with bad news from Corinth. Factions had formed in the church. There was rampant immorality, incest, lawsuits, and a host of other problems. Paul wrote 1 Corinthians to correct their patterns of sinful behavior.

Introduction (1 Corinthians 1:1-9)

Paul Addresses Problems in the Church (1 Corinthians 1:10–6:20)

Paul Answers Questions from the Church (1 Corinthians 7:1–16:4)

Conclusion (1 Corinthians 16:5-24)[3]

Paul begins 1 Corinthians by reminding the church about the second coming of Christ. The people had lost sight of their purpose as a church. Disunity was common as people began to associate with prominent religious leaders rather than Jesus. Even the Lord's Supper was corrupted when the shared meal became a party in which the rich received preferential treatment, drunkenness occurred, and some gorged on food while others had to go without.

The second half of the letter includes instructions for godly conduct. First Corinthians 12, for example, references spiritual gifts and how we are unified through diversity in the body of Christ. Chapter 14 deals with sign gifts and the way the church confused what happened at Pentecost with the ecstatic utterances of pagan practices. Chapter 15 refers to a group in the church who were denying the resurrection of Christ and addresses the evidence for Jesus appearing alive following his crucifixion. First Corinthians is an example of how knowing the occasion and context of the letter is key to understanding the meaning of the text. Paul is responding to specific abuses and problems in their church. Though the recipients of Paul's second letter to the Corinthians are the same, there are several important differences between the letters of 1 and 2 Corinthians.

1 Corinthians: Practical Advice for the Church	2 Corinthians: Personal Life of Paul
Paul addresses problems of conduct in the church	Paul shares personal stories
Focuses on issues	Focuses on answering accusations
Condemns worldliness	Warns about false teachers
Information about the Lord's Supper	Reasons for giving

Corinth was a challenging city for the early church. A wealthy and important city in Greece, it was known for its wickedness. Several schools of philosophy and art were present there, but immorality was common as the people pursued sinful pleasures of lust. In 2 Corinthians, Paul is concerned about the church's response to his first letter, which included several rebukes. He sends Titus to check on the people. Titus reports that most of the church received the first letter well, but a few doubted Paul's motives and even questioned his credentials as an apostle. In response, Paul's second letter to the Corinthians defends his authority and reminds the church to continue living holy lives.

Paul Explains His Actions and Defends His Ministry
(2 Corinthians 1–7)

Paul Defends the Collection for the Church in Jerusalem
(2 Corinthians 8–9)

Paul Defends His Apostolic Authority
(2 Corinthians 10–13)[4]

Galatians: Rescuing Troubled Churches

When Paul returns from Jerusalem to his home church in Antioch, he receives bad news from Galatia. Many of the people in the churches he helped plant during his first missionary journey have now been swept into false teaching.

A group called the "Judaizers" were trying to impose the laws of Judaism on Gentile converts to Christianity. They taught that those who wanted to follow Christ must first submit to the traditions of the Mosaic law, specifically the ritual of circumcision. These false teachers were likely the same Jewish leaders who stoned Paul at Lystra (Acts 14:19-20). They were influencing the people in Galatia, bringing confusion and doubt into the churches of the region. They were undercutting true doctrine, and undercutting Paul personally—both his authority and credibility.

Paul writes his letter to the Galatians to defend the doctrine of justification by faith by making it clear that no form of works can save. He also sends a stern, firm warning to the church about abandoning the true gospel of Jesus.

The book is structured around Paul's three primary concerns:

Paul Expresses Concerns over False Doctrine (Galatians 1–2)

Paul Defends the True Doctrine of the True Gospel
(Galatians 3–4)

Paul Shares the Freedom of the True Gospel (Galatians 5–6)

The point of this letter is to rescue the Galatian churches from the false teaching of Judaizers. In the first two chapters, Paul gives strong warnings to those who teach forms of legalism. He makes it clear we cannot earn God's salvation merely by keeping religious laws and traditions. Trying to earn God's favor through religious performance will only result in condemnation.

Paul writes that righteousness is not found in the law but in the person of Christ. Those who rely on the works of the law for salvation are cursed (Galatians 3:10-14). He states that it is foolish to turn away from the freedom of Christ and toward the bondage of legalism. The letter concludes with Paul's statement on freedom. We are not to abuse the privilege of Christian liberty. Rather, we should focus on the fruit of the Spirit over the works of the flesh. Paul's conclusion is simple: We boast in nothing except Christ Jesus (Galatians 6:14-15).

Ephesians: The Blessing of a Unified Church

The church at Ephesus was one of the more prominent congregations among the early churches, and it was also one of the healthiest of the churches Paul served. Ephesus was a commerce center in Asia Minor. Paul founded the church and spent three years teaching there. The tone of this letter is similar to that of Philippians. It is a message of encouragement. Paul writes to help the Christians of Ephesus understand the spiritual wealth they have in Christ. Throughout the letter, the themes of redemption, unity, and victory emerge—God lavishing upon his people the blessing of grace. Through Christ, people who are quite different can come together in unity. Ultimately, Christ gives victory over the powers of darkness.

In a pattern similar to Romans, the first half of Ephesians develops the doctrine of the church, while the second half applies the doctrine to our lives.

How God Gives Grace Lavishly (Ephesians 1–3)

How We Live Out Grace Accordingly (Ephesians 4–6)

Ephesians 1–3 focuses on the richness of God's grace. Chapters 4–6 bring to light how we should live because of this grace.

Paul begins the letter with a hymn of praise to God. In Ephesians 1, God is the subject of almost every verb. The purpose of Paul's praise is to point out that God is the sole provider of spiritual blessings. In the second chapter, Paul describes how Christ transfers us from a place of death to one of life. The third chapter develops the concept of a mystery revealed. The mystery to which Paul refers is that the gospel is available to everyone, and it is through the church that the message of Christ will go to all peoples. This revelation sets up the last three chapters, in which Paul describes how unity within the church comes through diversity. When Christ is central in the church and in the home, people who would otherwise not get along come together for God's glory.

Philippians: The Joy of Serving Together

God is faithful in giving us reliable joy rooted in his truth. God's joy is not fleeting but lasting. God's joy is what we need, not just want we want. God's joy is perfect, and it will never lead us astray. Paul writes a letter of encouragement to the Philippian church, and he reminds them of God's faithfulness. God always does what he says he will do, and it is always good.

This letter was written during Paul's imprisonment, probably while he was in Rome. Not coincidentally, Paul's most joyful letter comes from one of the darkest places. God reveals through this book how joy is possible in every circumstance.

The purpose of the letter is to thank the church at Philippi for their gifts and support in partnering with Paul for the gospel. Philippi is a big Roman city situated in modern-day northern Greece. The city was diverse and had a complex religious environment with many cults and religious practices. Egyptian, Roman, and Greek influences all converged in Philippi. The church there was primarily filled with Gentiles. They were generous and supported Paul financially. Paul deeply loved this church, and you can feel his emotions in the tone of the letter.

Finding Joy in Christ (Philippians 1:1-30)

Humble Joy through Christ (Philippians 2:1-18)

Friendly Joy in the Church (Philippians 2:19-30)

Genuine Joy of the Faith (Philippians 3:1-21)

Practical Joy in Giving (Philippians 4:1-23)

The first chapter begins with an internal struggle. Paul is in chains, but his soul is free. He realizes he may die, but he also knows being with Christ in heaven is better. Through the writing of this letter, Paul realizes God will *preserve* him as he *perseveres* in the faith.

Philippians 2 records a beautiful hymn of the early church. This hymn demonstrates the humility of Christ in coming to earth but also exalts Christ as King. Timothy and Epaphroditus are introduced as two examples of humility. In Philippians 3, Paul acknowledges the threat of the Judaizers, just as he had in his letter to the church at Galatia. He encourages the church to press toward God's goal and to stay focused on God's plans. Paul concludes the letter in the fourth chapter with more thankfulness for the generosity of the Philippians. Generosity is one of the key ways to cultivate joy.

Colossians: Protecting the Church from False Doctrine

This letter was written while Paul was in prison, around the same time he wrote his letter to the Ephesians. Ephesians and

Colossians are stylistically similar and contain a lot of church doctrine.

What Christ Has Done for Us (Colossians 1:1–2:25)

What We Should Do for Christ (Colossians 3:1–4:18)[5]

Paul never visited Colossae, but Ephesus was about ninety miles away. As Paul preached and taught in Ephesus, people from Colossae would travel back and forth to hear him, including the pastor of the church at Colossae, Epaphras. When Epaphras visited Paul and reported his concerns about misguided philosophical influences on the church, Paul wrote this letter in response.

Colossians is a work of both encouragement and warning. False teaching was creeping into the church, particularly the belief of Gnosticism, which was popular at the time. While Gnosticism is a complex philosophy, Paul's critique and response are clear in this letter. The Gnostics taught that intellectual assent leads to salvation, and God could be known through a logical thought process. According to Gnosticism, freedom from sin is not important. Rather, freedom from ignorance is the goal.

Gnostic Teaching	Paul's Answer
Salvation is obtained through wisdom.	Salvation is obtained through Christ living in us. (Colossians 1:27-29)
Jesus was not the Creator of the universe. He was created by God like the rest of creation.	Jesus is directly responsible for creating the universe. (Colossians 1:15-20)
Spiritual growth comes through asceticism, avoiding the joys of life and practicing self-denial.	Spiritual growth occurs because one is connected with Christ. (Colossians 2:16-19)

To combat Gnosticism, Paul gives a clear picture of Christ. In Colossians 1, Paul writes a hymn-like passage describing redemption through God's Son, Jesus. Paul then reveals the exaltation of the Son, who bears the Father's image. Paul is pointing to the centrality of Christ, who is eternal. Everything begins with Jesus, who was with God in the beginning.

In Colossians 2, Paul reminds the church that all true life comes from Jesus. He warns against "well-crafted arguments" of the Gnostics, and he reminds them to grow roots down into Jesus (Colossians 2:4, 7). In the third and fourth chapters, Paul reflects on how we are changed, both inwardly and outwardly, by Christ. Jesus redeems us from the inner struggle of sin and compels us to make the most of every opportunity to live for him.

1 and 2 Thessalonians: Standing Firm until Christ Returns

The background of the church at Thessalonica is found in Acts 17. Paul, Silas, and Timothy spent as little as three weeks in Thessalonica on their second missionary journey. In a short time, they started this church and created a stir in the city. As a result, the new church sent the three away, but the Holy Spirit began to work among the people.

In less than a month, a flourishing church began to grow. Paul was understandably concerned about the young church, so he sent Timothy back to them to see how they were doing. Timothy returned with a favorable report but noted issues that needed to be corrected.

Paul writes 1 Thessalonians to correct misunderstandings about the second coming of Christ. Some in the church were worried about those who had already died, fearing they would not be taken up to heaven. Others were so overwhelmed by the prospect of the Second Coming that they were neglecting their daily work. Paul writes to encourage the church to stand firm until Christ returns, and not to reject the daily routine that supports their families. Paul thanks the church for their zeal, reminisces about the start of the church, and writes about how he longs to see them. He encourages the church to avoid sin and place their hope in Christ.

The themes found in 1 Thessalonians carry forward into 2 Thessalonians, though there are differences.

1 Thessalonians	2 Thessalonians
Paul reminisces about their time together.	Paul encourages them to progress in the faith.
Paul teaches about the imminent return of Christ.	Paul corrects false teaching about Jesus' return.
Paul offers comfort and encouragement.	Paul offers assurance and correction.
Paul focuses on the church.	Paul focuses on the man of lawlessness.

The tone in 2 Thessalonians is more tense than that of 1 Thessalonians. Paul was upset that another person was using his name to propagate the false teaching that the Day of the Lord had already occurred, and the church was falling for the ruse. Additionally, some in the church did not heed Paul's advice in the first letter and were still not working.

In the first chapter of 2 Thessalonians, Paul comforts the church as they endure persecution. He reminds them about God's justice and their coming rest. In the second chapter, Paul corrects their misunderstandings about the end of days. He gives details about the man of lawlessness, who does the work of Satan. In Revelation, John will call this person the Antichrist. Both Paul and John remind the church that Jesus will conquer the Antichrist. The letter ends with instructions for believers in the third chapter. Paul requests prayer for the gospel to spread rapidly, and he again warns the church to stay away from those who are idle and do not work.

A Mix of Letters for a Diverse Church

While these letters were written by the same author, their subject matter and tone are often quite different. Through Paul, the Holy Spirit inspired a mix of letters for a diverse church. God knew churches today would need the joy of Philippians. God also understood other churches would need the correction of the Corinthian letters. These letters speak to the ups and downs of church life. While each letter was written because of a specific occasion during Paul's ministry, they are all relevant today. For example, not many Judaizers exist today, but the problem of legalism is still present. I doubt many churches today are abusing the Lord's Supper in the same way as the Corinthian church, but Paul's pathway of correction is still applicable to every congregation. These letters are more than historical windows into the early church. They also give us the encouragement, correction, and direction to navigate the climate in which our churches exist right now.

Paul's Pastoral Letters

Leading God's People Closer to Him

EVERY CHURCH NEEDS leadership. Paul wrote two letters to Timothy and one to Titus, explaining the relationship between leaders and the church. These books are often called the Pastoral Letters (or Epistles), but they are more than instructions for church leaders. Paul intended for everyone in the church to read the letters. In all three letters, instructions are given both to the pastors and to the congregation. Paul instructed Timothy and Titus *individually* but also wrote to the church *corporately* through the pastors. Do not make the mistake of thinking the pastoral letters are only for leaders. Though Paul wrote these books about church leaders, they also contain relevant and authoritative instruction for the governance of the church in any era and in any place.[1]

Paul mentions various leadership roles in his letters, among them pastor (Ephesians 4:11), bishop (1 Timothy 3:2, NKJV), and elder (Titus 1:5). The Greek word *poimen*, translated as *pastor*, refers to the shepherding role of church leaders. *Episkopos* is often translated *bishop*, *overseer*, or *church leader*. The third term, which is the one used most often, is *presbuteros*, which means *elder* or *leader*.

Though churches today have differing views on leadership and church governance, it's important to note one overriding biblical principle. The New Testament pattern of leadership in the church involves a plurality. Churches should have multiple leaders in place for accountability and equipping. For example, Paul told Titus to appoint elders in Crete (Titus 1:5). Each church was to have a group of elders leading the congregation. The top priority of these church leaders, then and now, is to guide people through God's Word and equip the congregation to make disciples.

First Timothy and Titus contain similar lists describing the qualifications of church leaders.[2] Though the characteristics can be categorized in various ways, three themes emerge: godly behavior, commitment to family, and selflessness.

First, a leader must have a proven pattern of godly behavior. The Greek word *anegkletos*, translated *blameless* or *above reproach*, is used to describe the lifestyle of an elder (Titus 1:6). Every leader is fallible, but all should maintain a consistent pattern of godliness.

The second theme of pastoral qualifications is a commitment to family. Marriage is a proving ground for leading the church. One who does not lead the home is not qualified to lead the church.

The third theme is a selfless focus on others. In the following list, notice how some terms in the pastoral letters can be categorized as not selfish (self-oriented) and some as selfless (others-oriented). The call to shepherd a church is a call to pour into others.

Not Selfish	Selfless
Not arrogant	Hospitable
Not hot-tempered	Loving goodness
Not a drunk	Sensible, righteous, holy
Not a bully	Self-controlled
Not greedy	Holding to the faithfulness of God's Word

Every church is different, each requiring leaders with different skill sets. The diversity of churches is necessary to reach a diverse world. All pastors, however, should lead God's people closer to him. No pastor should abuse power, promote self, or use authority to hide laziness. A hardworking, selfless pastor is a blessing to the church. And a church should, in return, bless such a pastor.

1 and 2 Timothy: Instructions for Pastors and Churches

Paul writes to Timothy about pastoral ministry. Timothy is like a son to Paul (1 Corinthians 4:17). Paul had taken Timothy with him as a companion on several missionary journeys and eventually left him in charge as a pastor of a church in Ephesus. Paul's letters portray Timothy as a godly leader (1 Timothy 6:11). His name appears about two dozen times in the New Testament. Paul wrote both 1 Timothy and 2 Timothy as an instruction manual for a young man in charge of a large church.

Timothy was the son of a Greek father and a Jewish mother (Acts 16:1). He had a good reputation; people spoke highly of him. Even though he was young, his track record was one of a growing ministry serving churches. His mother, Eunice, had a tremendous influence on his training, and she taught him the Scriptures (2 Timothy 1:5).

In many ways, 1 Timothy is a guidebook for young church leaders. Paul warns against empty speech and pursuing academic knowledge without applying it. He encourages Timothy to "fight well" and "cling to your faith," reminding him that leading a church is difficult and comes with many ups and downs (1 Timothy 1:18-19). Paul also admonishes churches to be careful about whom they place in leadership. Pastors should be proven, and positions of leadership should be reserved for those who qualify.

Paul begins his first letter to Timothy with a warning and follows it with specific directions for the church and the pastor.

Paul Warns against False Teaching (1 Timothy 1)

Paul Gives Directions for the Church (1 Timothy 2–3)

Paul Gives Directions for the Pastor (1 Timothy 4–6)

In the first chapter of 1 Timothy, Paul warns Timothy to watch out for those teaching a different doctrine. Without the foundation of a solid doctrine, the church will inevitably fall into the traps of sin. What we believe will determine our behavior.

Paul also encourages Timothy to "fight the good fight for the true faith" (1 Timothy 6:12). Not every potential battle in the church is worth fighting. The good fight is the one protecting the doctrine of the church.

Paul leaves Timothy at a tough church in a tough situation. Some church leaders are teaching false doctrine and leading people away from good doctrine. Before moving on to Macedonia, Paul removes some of those leaders from fellowship, but he expects Timothy to finish the job. The letter is addressed to Timothy rather than the church, perhaps so the false teachers will not see the letter and destroy it. Paul wants Timothy to replace these false teachers and train up new ones in their place. Paul's letter is firm but loving.

He does not write the typical greeting expressing thanksgiving as he does in other letters, and he leaves off his customary greetings to others at the end of the letter. The tone is serious because the situation calls for pointed leadership.

Paul's second letter to Timothy (circa AD 67) is the last letter Paul wrote, shortly before he was killed, likely by beheading. Paul knows the end is near. The church is in a mess. People are searching. They're scared. A few years earlier, Rome had burned under order of Nero—the wood shacks of the poor and the stone mansions of the rich were in ruins. To mask his guilt, Nero blamed the destruction on a pestilent little group called "Christians." Paul is chained. The church is persecuted. This backdrop is the context for 2 Timothy.

As an older pastor about to die, Paul wants to encourage his young protégé. The first letter to Timothy focused primarily on the church and the problems within the body. The second letter is directed primarily to Timothy. As a younger leader, Timothy is prone to waver. He can be too sensitive and too timid. Paul writes 2 Timothy to inspire both the pastor and the church to endure through persecution and persevere for the glory of God.

Endurance is the theme of 2 Timothy, and Paul leaves Timothy with the idea that a pastor's priority is to remain loyal to the gospel of Jesus above anything else. Be a faith contender and not a religious pretender.

The structure of the book follows his admonitions to Timothy.

Be Loyal (2 Timothy 1:1-18)

Be Strong (2 Timothy 2:1-13)

Be True (2 Timothy 2:14-19)

Be Pure (2 Timothy 2:20-26)

Be Firm (2 Timothy 3:1-9)

Be Wise (2 Timothy 3:10-17)

Be Persistent (2 Timothy 4:1-22)

Titus: Good Works for God's Glory

Paul's letter to Titus stresses the connection of pastors to churches. A healthy relationship between shepherds and churches primes God's people for good works in their communities. This letter was likely written around AD 65 between Paul's first and second stints in prison. Titus was a Gentile and one of Paul's companions. Paul left Titus on the island of Crete to keep the churches there in order. The post was not an easy one. Cretans had a bad reputation as a corrupt people. Titus would become the bishop of Crete. This letter was personal, but it was also meant to be read to the Christians on Crete.

The theme of good works is prevalent throughout the letter. Paul writes of being an example by doing good works, being eager to do good works, being ready to do good works, and devoting oneself to good works. The problem was "detestable" false teachers who claimed to know God but denied him by the way they lived (Titus 1:16). These teachers were ruining families in the churches and profiting off their false teaching. Paul challenges Titus to help others discern the false teaching, purge it from the church, and live in a way honoring to God.

The three-chapter structure of the book flows in progression from the pastor, to the church as a whole, to instructions for individual believers.

Good Pastors of the Church (Titus 1)

Good Teaching in the Church (Titus 2)

Good Works of the Believers (Titus 3)

The Cretan culture along with the false teachers made for a challenging environment for the churches on Crete. But God calls churches to be planted everywhere, including in places with tougher soil. Paul writes to remind them that the way they will stand out is through godliness. He writes to all generations in the church and encourages them to equip the young people. In a culture marked by corruption, greed, and excess, the church is called to respond with generosity and sacrifice.

Healthy Pastors and Healthy Churches

Timothy was one of Paul's closest companions. Titus was also mentored by Paul and traveled with him on missionary journeys. These two young men were now leading churches. Both pastors received valuable counsel from Paul, and the churches in Ephesus and Crete received important guidelines about the qualifications of church leadership. Paul's letters to Timothy and Titus are as relevant today as they were when they were written. Healthy pastors protect the church from false teaching, lead the church closer to God, and compel the church to fulfill the Great Commission. Healthy churches respond to good shepherding and equip all generations for God's work.

12

General Letters

The Church Matures

THE LAST SECTION of letters in the New Testament contains a variety of works by multiple authors. They include Philemon; Hebrews; James; 1 and 2 Peter; 1, 2, and 3 John; and Jude.

Though Philemon was written by Paul and the letter is sometimes categorized with Paul's other writings, the audience and subject matter set Philemon apart. It was written to an individual and contains instructions for dealing with a runaway slave.

The book of James, written by a half brother of Jesus, is one of the earliest writings in the New Testament. Hebrews, among the longer works, is rich in doctrine and Old Testament history, but there is much speculation as to who wrote the book. Peter contributed two letters, and the apostle John contributed three short writings. Jude was written by another half brother of Jesus.

The variety of authors and subject matter notwithstanding, these important letters demonstrate how the early church matured under the guidance of the Holy Spirit.

As we explore this final collection of New Testament letters, it's important to revisit the issue of hermeneutics, which I touched on in chapter 1. Hermeneutics is about uncovering the contemporary relevance of a specific text. Interpretation and exegesis help us understand Scripture in its past context. Hermeneutics helps us apply Scripture in the present. The New Testament letters present several hermeneutical challenges. Most churches today do not struggle with Judaizers or Gnostics, as was the case with the Galatian and Colossian churches. But what are we to do with the more controversial instructions from Paul about head coverings and holy kisses in his letters to the Corinthian church? Paul's letters to both Titus and Philemon give instructions regarding slavery, an abhorrent system of injustice and evil. How should contemporary readers—you and I!—apply these texts today?

Always begin with the intended meaning of the text. Ask what the text meant to the author and to the original audience. God's Word is unchanging, and the original meaning is still the meaning we must seek today. In the case of the Judaizers, studying a good commentary on Galatians will help with the historical backdrop of Paul's letter. Once you comprehend the intended meaning of the text, proper hermeneutics help you apply the passage to comparable situations in your context. For example, the specific problem of Judaizers requiring circumcision for salvation may not exist today, but legalism is still an issue for many churches. When reading the letters of the New Testament, every word is important, even the passages that were specific to the first-century context.

Philemon: The Gospel Heals All Relationships

This letter is Paul's shortest, written to Philemon, a member of the church at Colossae. One of Philemon's slaves, Onesimus, steals from him and then runs away. Onesimus makes his way to Rome, where he meets Paul. It's a divine encounter. Paul leads him to Christ, learns of his relationship to Philemon, and then sends Onesimus back home with a note, which is the book of Philemon. Unfortunately, slavery was common in the Roman Empire, and the issue of runaway slaves was common. Rome was a large city and an easy place to hide. In his sovereignty, God used this predicament to teach the church about forgiveness. If a relationship between a slave and his owner can be reconciled, then we all have hope with our relationships.

Paul is writing from prison (circa AD 60), and Philemon is a personal acquaintance. Philemon and his wife, Apphia, are wealthy and influential. Paul addresses two problems that need correcting. First and foremost, a freed family in Christ owns a slave and participates in an evil institution. Second, a slave seeks freedom in the wrong way and steals in the process. Onesimus could keep running. Philemon could go to the extreme of branding his slave to ensure he does not run away again. Neither option glorifies Christ. Both Philemon and Onesimus must extend forgiveness.

The doctrine of forgiveness in Philemon is not a theory; it is reality! Unforgiveness is a sin that disrupts the unity of the church. Because God has forgiven us freely and eternally, we can forgive one another here on earth. In this story, God took a situation that was intended for evil and used it for good. As with the

Old Testament book Jonah, we do not know how this story ends. Does forgiveness occur? Does Philemon free Onesimus? Since we have the letter, the assumption is that reconciliation happens. But we cannot know for certain. When the Bible leaves a story hanging, the implication is that we are to complete the story. The gospel heals all relationships, and the lesson of Philemon is that forgiveness can happen even for the most egregious of offenses.

Hebrews: A Better Way for the Church

Written by an unknown author to a Jewish audience (circa AD 65), this letter attempts to restart a church stalled in its progress. Members of the church were wavering in their faith, even thinking they had lost their Jewish heritage by accepting Christ. They were spiritually immature, and the writer desired to keep them from drifting.

The debate about authorship is one that garners a lot of attention among scholars. Some believe Paul wrote the letter, but it lacks his customary greeting. The Greek is more polished than Paul's, and the vocabulary is different. Some have speculated the writer to be Apollos, Peter, Barnabas, Luke, or others. While the debate continues, we will likely never know for sure.

Though Hebrews is often categorized as a letter, it may also have been a sermon (or a series of sermons). Hebrews includes many Old Testament quotes that would have been familiar to the original audience. The themes of "better" and "greater" emerge throughout Hebrews. The author sustains an argument that Christ is the culmination and fulfillment of the law. Jesus is both greater and better than the prophets, the angels, and even Moses (Hebrews 1:1-4; 3:1-10). The structure of the book reflects these themes:

The Greater Person of Jesus (Hebrews 1:1–8:6)

The Greater New Covenant of Jesus (Hebrews 8:7–10:39)

The Greater Life in Jesus (Hebrews 11:1–13:25)

The book of Hebrews reveals how the first covenant, the law, could not save. Its purpose was to reveal sin and point to the need of a Savior. God gave a new, greater covenant in Christ, who opened a better Tabernacle. The Tabernacle in the Old Testament was a picture, or symbol, of a greater sacrifice to come. Under the old covenant, the people had limited access to the Tabernacle, and the efficacy of sacrifices was temporary. In the new covenant, Christ is our priest, sacrificing himself to cleanse our sins forever. Through Jesus, we have immediate and eternal access to God. Knowing that Jesus' sacrifice gives direct access to God, the author of Hebrews encourages believers to be bold in their faith, to draw near to God, and to remain steadfast.

James: Developing a Faith that Works

Jesus' half brother James did not follow him until after the Resurrection. After Jesus appeared to him in a glorified state, James ultimately became the pastor of the church in Jerusalem (1 Corinthians 15:7). This letter is one of the earliest works in the New Testament, perhaps written around AD 50 but before AD 60.

James is an incredibly practical book, often referenced as the Proverbs of the New Testament. Written to a Jewish audience, James was possibly the first letter sent to Jewish Christians. At the time he wrote, believers were scattered and facing persecution. James encouraged them to *do* what God says, not just *listen* to God's Word (James 1:22-25). The faith James describes is one that works. Genuine faith inevitably leads to good works that honor

God. This letter is an early example of Jewish Christianity firmly rooted in the Old Testament but claiming Jesus as the Messiah.

The themes of James flow nicely from one chapter to the next. Each chapter represents a different facet of faith.

The Endurance of Faith (James 1)

The Works of Faith (James 2)

The Wisdom of Faith (James 3)

The Submission of Faith (James 4)

The Patience and Prayer of Faith (James 5)

The letter begins with the idea that trials are a joy. It is not the first reaction of many people to thank God for tough situations. Our perseverance under trials, however, grows our faith. Without seasons of testing, our faith would be weak. If God provided only an easy path, our faith would not grow. We gain a sense of victory when we overcome something difficult. James gives specific examples of how to grow, including controlling the tongue and avoiding the pitfall of pride. When bad behavior infects the church, chronic conflict destroys the people. The answer to the problem of conflict, according to James, is humility and submission to God's will. As you read James, note the numerous practical applications of growing in faith.

1 and 2 Peter: A Deeper Faith in Difficult Times

As one of the more powerful figures in the Gospels, Peter often captivates readers of the New Testament who gravitate toward the stories about him recorded in Matthew, Mark, Luke, and John. However, without Peter's two letters, we would not fully grasp how he matured in the faith and came to be one of the key leaders in the early church. He was originally named Simon, but Jesus gave him the new name Peter (or Cephas in Aramaic). He was a Jewish fisherman and the brother of Andrew. As part of the inner circle of disciples with James and John, Peter became a spokesperson for the apostles. The first twelve chapters in Acts focus on his ministry.

The theme of holiness is seen in the structure of 1 Peter, while 2 Peter focuses on the spiritual growth and discernment of the believer.

Living a Holy Life in God's Family (1 Peter 1:1–2:10)

Living a Holy Life in Your Individual Context (1 Peter 2:11–3:7)

Living a Holy Life in the Face of Opposition (1 Peter 3:8–5:14)

Growing in Godliness (2 Peter 1:1-11)

Relying on God's Word as Truth (2 Peter 1:12-21)

Condemning False Teachers (2 Peter 2:1-22)

Preparing for Jesus to Return (2 Peter 3:1-18)

First Peter was written sometime between AD 60 and 65 to Gentile Christians dispersed throughout Rome during the early phases of church persecution. Like James, Peter encourages the church to endure trials with joy as they prove their faith to be genuine (1 Peter 1:6-7). Later he adds, "It is better to suffer for doing good . . . than to suffer for doing wrong!" (1 Peter 3:17).

In the second chapter, Peter compares Jesus to a cornerstone.

There are two choices: either build your life on him or stumble over him and fall tragically into condemnation.

In his first letter, Peter encourages believers to live in a godly way even in the face of hostility. In his second letter, Peter shifts the focus slightly and writes about how a shallow faith will lead to a superficial life. The first letter focuses on the outside dangers to the church through persecution. The second letter is a warning against the inside threat of false doctrine.

1 Peter	2 Peter
Encouragement for those suffering persecution	Warning to avoid false teachers
Danger outside the church (persecution)	Danger inside the church (false doctrine)
Perseverance through trials	Awareness of dangerous teaching

Because of stylistic differences between the two letters, there is some controversy concerning the authorship of 2 Peter. The grammar and Greek of 1 Peter are far superior to those of 2 Peter. Because the second letter claims Peter as the author, these differences are a significant issue but are not insurmountable. One explanation is that Peter wrote the second letter himself. Since he spoke Aramaic, his Greek would not have been as good. Peter probably wrote his first letter with the help of a literary assistant, Silas, who is mentioned at the end of the letter (1 Peter 5:12).

1, 2, and 3 John: Love, Truth, and Hospitality

Letters do not need to be long to be genuine. John writes three short letters, but the love contained in them is immense. Each of these letters has a different perspective on the overarching theme of love.

God's Love through the Assurance of Salvation (1 John)

God's Love through His Truth (2 John)

God's Love through Our Hospitality (3 John)

John's first letter is written to Christians at large. It is intended to be a companion to John's Gospel. John was the beloved disciple of Jesus and part of the inner circle of disciples, along with Peter and James. John's first letter is longer than his other two, and he covers several topics. The most prevalent theme is the assurance of salvation. John's Gospel reveals *how* someone can be saved. John's first letter demonstrates how to *know* you are saved. This letter was written between AD 85 and 95, following Jerusalem's fall to the Romans in AD 70. John writes from Ephesus, but the believers are scattered throughout the empire. He is older, and his tone is fatherly. Terms such as "dear children" and "friends" point to John's deep love. Throughout the letter, John addresses fundamental Christian beliefs and points to the way believers should live.

Second John is a private correspondence written to an unknown Christian woman. In fact, it is the only book in the Bible addressed to a woman. John encountered her children and was compelled to write her. The children were living in God's truth, and John wrote to encourage her. The theme of truth appears several times in the short letter.

Third John was written to a generous friend named Gaius. He is noted for his hospitality, especially in hosting traveling preachers. John encouraged him to continue these acts of hospitality. The theme of 3 John is that a culture of hospitality is critical to the spread of the gospel. It was the case then, and it remains true today.

Jude: Contending for the Faith

Like James, Jude was a half brother of Jesus. He, too, was converted following the Resurrection. This book, written between AD 60 and 80, is completely devoted to the issue of apostasy. Generally, apostasy is a movement away from a belief system. Those who commit apostasy rebel against views they formerly held. In Jude, a group of false teachers are working behind the scenes to derail the church. They are stealthy, having "wormed their way" into the church unnoticed (Jude 1:4).

Jude begins with a warning about false teachers and ends the short letter with a call to faithfulness.

A Warning about the Dangers of False Teachers (Jude 1:1-16)

A Call to Remain Faithful to Christ (Jude 1:17-25)

Jude writes to warn his readers that these false teachers may look and act like shepherds but are evil, and he compares them to Old Testament figures who abandoned God's will. In Jude 1:12-13, he uses several analogies to point out the empty promises of their false teaching:

dangerous reefs: Bad doctrine shipwrecks faith.

shameless shepherds: False teachers are selfish and care only for themselves.

waterless clouds: Bad doctrine makes false promises.

trees in autumn: False teachers offer only barrenness.

wild waves: Bad doctrine wastes energy and has a dangerous undertow.

wandering stars: False teachers lead people away from the true light.

The answer to false teaching is a church equipped to contend for the faith. Jude encourages believers to build each other up and to pray in the Holy Spirit's power. They are to stay focused on God's love and not divisiveness. For those who are influenced by bad doctrine, Jude encourages the church to show mercy and take the initiative to save them from making poor decisions.

Letters for a Maturing Church

Every new believer begins at a point of immaturity. Salvation is God's work to save a person, but sanctification is the Spirit's work to grow a believer. While the variety of subjects and authors in the general letters may initially seem to create a jumble of lessons, what ties them together is their common focus on the maturation and growth of people in the church. Philemon contains a beautiful lesson on forgiveness. Hebrews demonstrates that the new covenant is necessary for salvation. James offers practical advice for growing in faith. The books of 1 and 2 Peter warn of potential dangers, and Jude warns of apostasy. John's three letters speak to hospitality and how to demonstrate love to others. Immensely relatable, these letters set up the final book of the Bible, Revelation, which is a masterful and climactic finish to God's story that began in Genesis.

Revelation

The Perfect Ending to God's Story

GOD HAS THE POWER to make things right. He *will* make things right, and Revelation is God's promise of a perfect ending to his grand story. What began in Genesis is completed in the book of Revelation. Genesis describes the creation of heaven and earth. Revelation describes a new heaven and a new earth. What begins with the marriage of the first Adam is completed in the marriage feast of the Lamb with the second Adam, Jesus Christ. Satan appears in the beginning of Genesis, but at the end of Revelation, he is destroyed. God's first paradise, the Garden of Eden, was destroyed with our sin. The Bible ends with a restored paradise for everyone who places faith in Christ.

John is the author of Revelation. He was the pastor of the church at Ephesus but is now banished to the island of Patmos. Church tradition teaches he was boiled alive during a time of church persecution but managed to survive. He was among the youngest disciples and lived to be the oldest, passing away in his mid-nineties. John writes Revelation on Patmos circa AD 90–95. While on the island, John is forced to work at hard labor, probably in the mines and quarries. In the first verse of Revelation, John reveals that Jesus communicated to him through an angel. With newfound hope, John records Jesus' words through the messenger.

Revelation is the only book of prophecy in the New Testament. Other books contain prophecy, but Revelation stands alone as an entire book devoted to the genre. The prophecy of Revelation helps us understand God's work in the future in order to speak God's word to the people in the present.[1] God promises a special blessing to those who read the book (Revelation 1:3). John records how Christ ultimately defeats evil and remedies all injustices. Satan does not want you to read it! This reason alone is enough to start plumbing the depths of Revelation.

The Apocalyptic Genre of Revelation

Unfortunately, too many read Revelation as a riddle instead of as an unveiling. Is the book hard to understand? Yes, it is. But God is not trying to trick you with the style of writing. No doubt, there are some bizarre happenings in Revelation. The book is part of the apocalyptic literature of the era and contains more than three hundred symbols. The style appeared around the second century BC as a response to oppression, but Revelation is not the only book written in this style. There are other historical examples. The book is both apocalyptic in style and prophetic in tone.

Apocalyptic literature at the time focused on God's interventions at the end of days. The purpose was to reveal God's plan to stop injustice and offer restoration to the persecuted. What sets Revelation apart from other prophetic writings is the primary form of communication. In the Old Testament, prophets would speak or preach their messages. In Revelation, John writes his message. Apocalyptic literature places primary emphasis on the cataclysmic events that occur at the end of time, while prophetic messages also focus on near-term future events. Many of the apocalyptic writers during John's time had a more pessimistic tone, but John writes with hope. As an eyewitness to the resurrected Jesus, John knows the power of his Savior. While the end of days is preceded by a series of tragic events, God's redemption story concludes with the glorification of his followers.

The Context and Theme of Revelation

The church is facing persecution and an inevitable clash with the state. In this case, the state is the Roman Empire in the first century. The Roman emperor was "lord" over everyone. Most likely, the backdrop to Revelation is the reign of Domitian. John's exile and the martyrdom of Antipas, a "faithful witness," are just the beginning of a battle between the advancing gospel and the power structure of the state (Revelation 2:13). The conflict between the church and Rome brings context to an even greater conflict—the battle between God and Satan. John writes to remind the church that God not only gives victory today through faith in Jesus Christ, but God also brings ultimate victory over evil through the culmination of events that occur in the future.

We cannot know everything about the future through Revelation. What the book does unveil, however, is that God knows everything, and we can trust him. Three key lessons emerge from Revelation. First, Christ will return suddenly and visibly, as well as literally in human form. Jesus' return will be unexpected, and there is no way for us to know the exact time and date. Second, the church, as God's people, should anticipate Christ's second coming. While we cannot know the timing, we should be on the lookout, living righteously today in anticipation for what will happen in the future. Third, when Christ returns, he will bring judgment on those who deny him and reward those who follow him. As you read Revelation, the details of symbolic imagery are important, but do not miss these grand themes. John's primary objective is to bring the church closer to Jesus through his visions of the end times.

Because Christ will return, we must live in readiness. Jesus controls history. Indeed, he is Lord over history. And he will bring history to its proper conclusion. John uses the concept of a sacrificial lamb to encourage his readers. Jesus is the sacrificial lamb, and John mentions this connection over twenty times in Revelation. In his Gospel, John often referred to Jesus as the Good Shepherd. The consistent use of "sheep" in the Bible to describe Christ's followers is not exactly a compliment. Sheep are slow and defenseless. They require constant watch and care. Sheep, however, are also quite valuable. Their wool, skin, and meat were necessities in John's culture. The lesson is simple. We are valuable to God, but we must also understand how helpless we are on our own.

Jesus became like a lamb—slaughtered—to save the sheep. But why a lamb? Why this connection to sheep? Unlike other sacrificial animals, a lamb does not fight back. Jesus was a willing sacrifice for us. Isaiah prophesied about the silence of the lamb, silent before shearers (Isaiah 53:7). John records the thunderous worship of a heavenly chorus: "Worthy is the Lamb who was slaughtered" (Revelation 5:12). The Lamb was silent when he sacrificed himself for us. Revelation is a reminder that we, the church, need to be loud for Jesus. Even as persecution ravages the church, or even as we approach the end of days, the church must be a loud voice for the message of the sacrificial Lamb.

The Different Views of Revelation

As you read Revelation, it is important to be aware of some differences in how scholars and theologians explain the book. Unfortunately, some Christians don't give proper attention to eschatology (the study of the end of days) because of the controversies and dogmatism surrounding the interpretation of Revelation. What happens to us at the end of our lives? What happens to the earth at the end of time? We should not overlook these questions. At the same time, we should not be so dogmatic as to claim our view of eschatology to be the only possible true version. I believe part of the blessing God gives to readers of Revelation is the discovery of new depths and riches every time we read it.

There are four dominant views of Revelation: *preterist*, *historicist*, *idealist*, and *futurist*.

The Preterist View

This view holds that many of the prophecies in Revelation were fulfilled in the first century. According to the preterist understanding, Revelation is not so much a calendar of future events but rather a commentary on events at the time. Those who are preterists read Revelation more like one of Paul's letters, written to a particular people in a particular place and time. The strength of this view involves the context of John's letter. He did not write in a vacuum, and the narrative was no doubt influenced by what was happening as he wrote. Revelation is often read in a way that detaches John's letter from his context. The preterist view restores this connection. The weakness of this view is that it tends to restrict the message of the book too much. The prophecies in Revelation extend beyond the first century, and not everything John wrote was limited to the near future.

The Historicist View

Popular during the Middle Ages, this view understood Revelation as a progression of history in western Europe. The symbols in Revelation were often connected to popes, kings, wars, and other events and leaders of Europe. The historicist viewpoint connected patterns in Revelation to the patterns within the context of the Middle Ages. The wide influence of this view is why Luther, Calvin, and other reformers often equated the harlot of Babylon with the Catholic popes of their eras. While this view is largely absent today, its influence remains. The temptation still exists to view Revelation through a narrow lens of our own context and place. Some Christians in the United States, for example, try to connect a certain president to being the Antichrist, or a government order or program to some of the symbols in Revelation. While the events in Revelation will eventually unfold at some time and place, we should not default to believing these happenings will occur around us and in our time.

The Idealist View

In many ways, this view is the opposite of the historicist view. Those who hold to the idealist view believe Revelation has less to do with events in time and more to do with a symbolic narrative portraying a final battle of good and evil. Many early church fathers held to this view, including Augustine, who, in his work *City of God*, posited that the millennium was not a literal thousand years but rather a symbolic way of referring to the spiritual reign. The strength of this view is that Revelation is full of symbols, and not all of them are tied to specific events. However, the converse becomes its weakness. Portions of Revelation are tied to actual future events. The idealist view helps the reader understand the symbolic elements of John's book, but it can also lack clarity when reading Revelation with future events in mind.

The Futurist View

This view became extraordinarily popular in the twentieth century and has dominated literature over the last hundred years. The futurist sees Revelation 4–22 as pertaining to future events, but there is much disagreement as to how these future events unfold. Some hold to a more dispensational understanding of Revelation, that the book records specific time periods during which everything unfolds. Others who hold this view are not as rigid as to how the future becomes reality.

The varying viewpoints of Revelation should not discourage you from studying this amazing book. Use good commentaries and read with discernment. No matter which view you hold, be humble about your study. There are clearly some symbolic elements to the book. Satan is not *literally* a red dragon, for example. The symbolism, however, should not take away from reading the book literally. Satan *does* exist, after all!

The Imagery of Revelation

One of the most engaging aspects of this great book is how John uses imagery. Numbers, colors, and sounds make for a vivid experience when reading Revelation. Remember what Paul tells Timothy: that all of Scripture is useful (2 Timothy 3:16). When you encounter the wild and even bizarre imagery in Revelation, it is good and useful to you. Do not dismiss this imagery, but do not elevate it above the rest of Scripture. This principle also applies to the numbers, colors, and sounds in John's letter.

When reading numbers, a few good rules of thumb are helpful. Fractions can represent incompleteness. Four often represents the earth as a reference to the four directions—north, south, east, and west. Five can represent punishment, and six can represent evil or incompleteness. Seven can depict perfection, often pointing to God in heaven. Ten and twelve can represent completeness or fullness. When the Beast rises out of the sea in Revelation 13:1, for example, it has seven heads and ten horns. This number represents the full power that Satan will have for a time. The seven heads are symbolic of complete blasphemy against God.

Colors are also a key part of imagery in Revelation. White can represent purity. Emerald green can represent life, while pale green depicts death. Gold shows value, and red is symbolic of sin. Black can foretell death and famine. As you read, notice how colors are associated with particular images and events.

Sounds are also prominent in Revelation and often overlooked. They are meant to grab our attention in the way we might use boldface or underlining to emphasize a portion of text. In Revelation, Jesus speaks loudly like a trumpet. The cries of the martyrs in chapter 6 make for a difficult read. When the seventh seal is opened in chapter 8, silence becomes a cacophony of noise. The loudest noise is reserved for the end of the book. When the vast crowd of heaven starts to worship Jesus in chapter 19, the overpowering roar sounds like the crashing of waves and the cracking of thunder.

The Visions of Revelation

There are several ways to structure the book of Revelation, one of which is by the four visions.

Vision 1 (Revelation 1:9–3:22)

Vision 2 (Revelation 4:1–16:21)

Vision 3 (Revelation 17:1–21:8)

Vision 4 (Revelation 21:9–22:4)

The first vision occurs on Patmos (Revelation 1:9–3:22). God tells John to write letters to seven churches. John gives these churches both commendations and warnings. This section of Revelation is one of the more familiar and contains a lot of application for congregations today.

The Church at Ephesus: Abandoned their first love

The Church at Smyrna: Facing persecution and poverty

The Church at Pergamum: Tolerating sin

The Church at Thyatira: The prosperous but compromised church

The Church at Sardis: The lifeless and powerless church

The Church at Philadelphia: The obedient, persevering church

The Church at Laodicea: The lukewarm church

God moves John from the island of Patmos to heaven for the second vision (Revelation 4:1–16:21). The geographic move from Patmos to heaven represents a thematic shift away from the analysis of the current state of the churches to a vision of future events. John is summoned to the throne room of heaven. In the first vision, his viewpoint is from earth. In the second vision, his viewpoint is from heaven. No longer is he on earth's time but rather on God's time.

The second vision includes the seven-sealed scroll, which demonstrates the problem of inaccessibility to God's throne. Then the seven seals and seven trumpets reveal a process of judgment in which a series of catastrophic events show God's wrath. John watches as

Jesus opens the seals and releases judgment. The earth experiences burning, pollution, and torment. Seven symbolic episodes are involved in this dramatic experience. The second vision ends with seven bowls filled with judgments and plagues. These bowls of judgments are similar to the trumpet judgments but with more intensity.

As the vision from heaven ends, the third vision begins (Revelation 17:1–21:8). God moves John from the heavenly realm to the desert. This section describes God's triumph. The descriptions of wrath move into the assurance of God's sovereignty. God will judge the wicked and reward the righteous. The nations assemble to worship Jesus, and the people begin to gather for the marriage feast of the Lamb. Then Jesus, the rider on the white horse, defeats evil. Satan is bound as God issues final judgment. The third vision ends with a new heaven and a new earth.

The fourth and final vision (Revelation 21:9–22:4) moves John from the desert to a mountain. In this vision, John describes a glorified church and a new Jerusalem. Justice is now complete, and the rewards of faith are distributed. The theme around the number seven continues as seven new items are introduced: a new heaven, new earth, new Jerusalem, new light, new river, new mountain, and new tree of life—a whole new paradise! Most importantly, God is there.

Unlocking the Meaning of Revelation

The more you study the last book of the Bible, the more beautiful it becomes. The first reading is intense, and it can be a struggle to understand the vivid imagery and symbolic elements of this apocalyptic literature. The promise of Revelation, however, is one of blessing. God blesses in the moment as we read and gives us assurance of future blessings that come in the culmination of the end of days.

Can Christ return at any moment? Some believe certain events in Revelation must take place first, and we must be on the lookout for the fulfillment. Others believe Christ can fulfill these events at any point and may return at any time. The unlocking of Revelation is not so much about figuring out these future events as it is an entreaty to prepare our own souls. What Revelation teaches is that we must be ready. It's a question we all need to ask: "Am I ready for Christ's return?" If not, perhaps it's time to read John's book with a fresh set of eyes.

Your Commitment
to God's Word

REMEMBER THE CHINESE believers I mentioned in the introduction? They wept together after receiving their own personal copies of the Bible. Remember what one Chinese woman said?

"This is what we needed most."

We have journeyed through every book of the Bible. I hope you now have a greater appreciation of God's purpose for your life. The whole Bible is for your whole life. It's what you need most.

Your next step involves commitment.

Three Right-Now Actions to Start Your Commitment

A church member called me one evening and asked if I would go with him to visit a couple he considered friends. It was late, a time of night I'm not usually out and about, and in a part of town I usually don't frequent. But I agreed to go.

When we walked into their home, I could sense their distress. The husband and wife were lucid but clearly agitated. They were seated in the only two chairs in the room. My friend and I stood and listened as they poured out their troubles.

After an hour of hearing about their spiritual oppression, my friend pointed to a Bible that was sitting open by the television. "It's open to the same page as the last time I was here," he said.

The couple had spoken highly of the Bible, said they believed the Bible and wanted to follow what was in the Bible, but it was obvious they weren't spending any time *reading* the Bible.

The Bible is not a lucky charm. It's not an amulet to ward off dark and evil spirits. Having a Bible on your coffee table or in your backpack will do *nothing* for you unless you read it. Downloading a Bible app onto your phone is a good idea, but there's no spiritual value unless you *read* it.

According to a national research study, the number one way in which people grow spiritually is through daily Bible reading. Unfortunately, only 35 percent of active churchgoers say they study the Bible at least once a week.[1] Ask anyone if they want to be healthier spiritually, and the likely answer will be *yes*. But you have to do what it takes to make that happen. Reading your Bible is the best path to spiritual maturity. The best decision you can make is to open your Bible every day and read God's Word.

Here are three action steps to jump-start your commitment.

Make your Bible visible. The probability is high that if you're reading this book—which is about understanding the Bible—you own a copy of God's Word. Go get it right now. Far too often, when something is out of sight it is out of mind. Place your Bible in a spot where you will see it regularly. If your Bible is on your phone, then make the app icon the first thing you see when you unlock the screen. We need visible reminders of the importance of reading the Bible. Make your actual Bible the visible reminder to read it.

Put Bible reading on your calendar. Now that you have the Bible placed prominently as a reminder to read it, open your calendar. I use a digital calendar. My wife uses a paper calendar.[2] Whatever version of a calendar you have, block time on it for the spiritual discipline of reading your Bible. Schedule a time right now. Make reading your Bible *the* priority in your day. I prefer to read in the afternoons or evenings. Your time may be mornings. Pick a time you know will work for you.

Follow a Bible reading plan. There are an abundance of Bible reading plans to choose from. A quick internet search will reveal several good ones. But the reading plan itself is secondary to identifying a certain portion of text to read each day or a set amount of time to read each day. How incredible if you are inspired to read for an hour a day or through the Bible in a year! Most people, however, find it challenging to start with such a large endeavor. There is no shame in starting with five minutes a day of Bible reading. Or in reading a chapter a day in your favorite book of the Bible. I'm a pastor. My job is to study the Bible. For devotional time, I don't utilize the Bible reading plans that cover all of Scripture in a year. The reason is simple—I prefer to meditate on a chapter at a time for my daily reading. I also like to delve deep into the Psalms and Proverbs. Sometimes I will pray through one proverb for my devotional and spend ten or twenty minutes memorizing a verse or two. The best way to start reading your Bible is to pick a portion of text (such as a chapter or a page) or timeframe (a set number of minutes) you know you can accomplish. Don't set yourself up to fail. It's better to read God's Word for five minutes a day than not at all!

Developing a Deeper and More Enduring Commitment

Once you have a consistent habit of reading God's Word, you can develop a deeper connection over time. Christian commitment means reading the Bible to know God, praying the Bible to love God, and applying the Bible to serve God. You do not make a commitment to God's Word in isolation. An enduring love of God's Word happens within the context of the church community, within the discipline of worship, and through memorization and meditation.

God's Word within the Church Community

The image of a bride is a powerful one—so powerful that God compares the church to a bride. In the Bible, the people of God are the bride. Jesus is the groom. When God completes his Kingdom, the entire church (the bride) will experience heaven with Jesus (the groom). Scripture is clear. We are not to attempt the Christian life in isolation. The commitment to God's Word requires the community of God, the church.

Sometimes, all you need to know is that you're not alone. Spiritually, you don't grow in isolation. Nobody can grow alone. It takes others. The selflessness of the early church—their radically sacrificial nature—was striking to the people in their community. But this was not some version of silly utopianism. Rather, it was a spiritual willingness to sacrifice for those in need. In the early church, it seems as if daily life was an interruption to their commitment to God's Word. Today, we treat God's Word as if it is an interruption to daily life.

If you love Jesus, the groom, then you must also love his bride, the church. The writer of Hebrews says we are to "motivate one another to acts of love and good works," and to make sure we do not "neglect our meeting together" as the church (Hebrews 10:24-25). The phrase from Hebrews in the original Greek implies irritating one another—not in the sense of annoyance, but for accountability. Much as sandpaper helps a carpenter finish a fine piece of furniture, we must be refined by the grit of Christian accountability. Without accountability, you will lack completion. The Bible is intended to be studied within the community of the church. You simply will not grow as God desires if you study the Bible alone and without the help of other Christians.

God's Word and the Discipline of Worship

One of the enduring themes of the Bible is God's glory. Because God deserves all glory, we worship him. What makes us holy and acceptable in worship is our willingness to give God all of who we are (Romans 12:1). When we *give* in worship, we *get* God. One of the marks of a healthy believer is a desire for more of God, not just a desire for the good things he gives.

Have you ever driven down the road, zoned out, and arrived at a place by sheer routine? Then you realized you were not at the place you intended to go. Habit got you there. When my brother lived in Miami, his townhome was by the main rail lines. When I visited in his home after he first moved in, we stopped our conversation every few minutes when the trains passed because the noise and vibration was hard to ignore. However, it wasn't long until we stopped noticing the trains at all. Routine made us numb to the obvious. How do we avoid going through the motions and becoming numb to God's Word? The answer is regular corporate worship with the bride of Christ. Disciplined worshipers are often invigorated Bible readers.

God's Word—Memorization and Meditation

Reading God's Word is beneficial but experiencing the richness of Scripture occurs through memorization and meditation. Simply reading something does not mean you absorb it. Of course, this reality applies to the Bible. You should hear God's Word read in corporate worship. You should make personal time to read God's Word. You should study God's Word with other believers in the context of the church. But memorizing and meditating on God's Word helps you retain it and apply it over the long term.

Memorizing Bible verses takes time and intentional effort. You don't accidentally memorize Scripture. The effort is purposeful. How do you memorize Scripture? Write out verses in repetition. Say these verses out loud several times. Make reminder cards with the verses printed on them and place these cards where you will see them regularly in your home.

The word *meditation* can have a negative connotation within the Christian community. However, biblical meditation is simply the process of thinking deeply on Scripture and prayerfully asking God to reveal his reality. One meditation technique is to pray through a passage of Scripture. As you read each word and each verse, say a short prayer to God about what you are learning. Honor and glorify him as you read. Another technique involves writing out several questions about a passage, then carefully researching the answer to these questions with trusted resources. Meditating on the Bible involves prayer and study. Connecting to God's Word with these techniques helps build perseverance of the faith.

God's Story Revealed to You

Occasional encounters with God's Word are better than no encounters, but consistent spiritual growth requires an enduring commitment to Scripture. The goal is to go long and deep, not brief and shallow. You should not read the Bible the way you scan news headlines. Read the Bible as if it is a letter from a loved one explaining the history and backstory of your family. You would keep such a letter, cherish it, and share the content with the next generation. Learn to soak in every word in the Bible because every word will have an impact on your life.

The Bible is God's story revealed to you. Everything God wants you to know about him is contained in the sixty-six books of the Bible. Every verse and all the words point to God's plan of redemption through Jesus. As you meditate, memorize, and study, the Holy Spirit will guide you. When you make the commitment to go deep into the meaning of Scripture, God will honor your passion.

God does not speak imprecisely. If God can speak falsely, then he has the capacity to fail. And if God can fail, then we should not trust him or his Word. Thankfully, Scripture is both inspired and infallible. The Bible comes from a perfect God who speaks with perfect precision. God's Word will not lead you astray. We are not more accurate than God, and the only way we can know how to live is through the Bible. Scripture is sufficient, and we don't have to search for God. Through the Bible, God has revealed to us all that he wants us to know so we can live for him. Ultimate authority rests with God's Word. If there were no written record from God, then we would not have any assurance of what he wants from us.

The Bible will never deceive. God cannot lie (Hebrews 6:18). Life experience, good advice, and learning from others are all important, but what you gather from others and on your own must be validated by God's Word. The sixty-six books of the Bible are unlike any other. You can read them for clarity. You can study them for guidance. You can meditate on them to find fulfillment. Spiritual discernment is not correlated to intellectual capacity.

God provides clarity to all who go deep into his Word. Don't make searching for God harder than it needs to be. Any person genuinely seeking God in his Word can know truth and experience the guidance of the Holy Spirit.

This is God's Word. It is without error. It will not lead you astray. It is all you need for life. It is the authority over everything else. God revealed his story to you. There is only one response: Commit all of who you are to him.

Notes

INTRODUCTION: THE WHOLE BIBLE FOR YOUR WHOLE LIFE

1. "Missionary Footage Captures Emotion of Chinese Christians Receiving Bibles for the First Time," March 17, 2014, YouTube video, 0:56, https://www.youtube.com/watch?v=CkXDcdMNE-I.

2. Galileo Galilei, "Letters on Sunspots," in *Discoveries and Opinions of Galileo*, trans. Stillman Drake, (New York: Doubleday Anchor, 1957), 77.

3. Perhaps you have already picked up on two terms: *Bible* and *Scripture*. What's the difference? The word *Scripture* literally means "the writings." It refers to what was once a collection of separate scrolls, which is the form in which the texts were originally written. It wasn't practical to put all of God's Word onto one scroll as it would have been unwieldy and difficult to read. The word *Bible* came into use more often after the bound book was invented. For the first time, all the scrolls could be printed in a single volume. We will use these terms interchangeably throughout the book.

CHAPTER 1: UNDERSTANDING THE BEGINNING

1. Clinton E. Arnold, *How We Got the Bible: A Visual Journey* (Grand Rapids: Zondervan, 2008), 14.

2. Arnold, *How We Got the Bible*, 16–17.

3. Some editions of the Bible include the fourteen books of the Apocrypha with the Old Testament. These books were written primarily during the four hundred years that elapsed between the end of the Old Testament and the beginning of the New Testament. They are not accepted as canonical, but they provide a historical backdrop to the time period.

4. *Foxe's Book of Martyrs* (London: Knight and Son, 1856), 488.

5. "Bible Translations Bestsellers, January 2020," Evangelical Christian Publishers Association, January 2020, https://christianbookexpo.com /bestseller/translations.php?id=0120.

6. *The Message* is more of a paraphrase than most dynamic equivalent translations, and it is sometimes described as a "free translation" because it is less concerned with using the exact wording from the originals.

7. The term *old* in reference to God's covenant in the Old Testament does not mean outdated. Nor does the term *new* in reference to the New Testament mean better.

8. George H. Guthrie, *Read the Bible for Life: Your Guide to Understanding and Living God's Word* (Nashville: Broadman and Holman, 2011), 226.

CHAPTER 2: GOD'S LAW

1. Gordon J. Wenham, *Word Biblical Commentary: Genesis 1–15* (Waco: Word, 1987), xxii.

2. Henrietta Mears, *What the Bible Is All About: Bible Handbook* (Ventura, CA: Regal Books, 1999), 39.

CHAPTER 3: ISRAEL'S HISTORY

1. Eugene H. Merrill, *Kingdom of Priests: A History of Old Testament Israel*, second edition (Grand Rapids: Baker Academic, 2008), 171.

2. Stephen J. Bramer, "Kinsman-Redeemer," *Baker's Evangelical Dictionary of Biblical Theology*, Bible Study Tools, https://www.biblestudytools.com /dictionaries/bakers-evangelical-dictionary/kinsman-redeemer.html.

CHAPTER 4: THE POST-EXILIC PERIOD

1. Gleason L. Archer, *A Survey of Old Testament Introduction* (Chicago: Moody, 1994), 449.

2. Alan B. Stringfellow, *Through the Bible in One Year: A 52-Lesson Introduction to the 66 Books of the Bible* (Tulsa: Virgil W. Hensley, 1978), 54.

CHAPTER 5: POETRY AND WISDOM

1. Some translations refer to the book as Song of Solomon.

2. Norman L. Geisler, *A Popular Survey of the Old Testament* (Grand Rapids: Baker, 1989), 183.

3. Geisler, *A Popular Survey of the Old Testament*, 182–183.

4. Geisler, *A Popular Survey of the Old Testament*, 183.

CHAPTER 6: PSALMS

1. C. Hassell Bullock, *Encountering the Book of Psalms: A Literary and Theological Introduction* (Grand Rapids: Baker Academic, 2001), 86.

NOTES

CHAPTER 7: THE MAJOR PROPHETS

1. When God commanded Ezekiel to use dried human dung, Ezekiel protested that he had never defiled himself with anything forbidden by Jewish law. God then relented and permitted him to use cow dung (Ezekiel 4:12-15).
2. For examples of New Testament references to Jesus as prophet, priest, and king, see Matthew 21:11; John 6:14; Hebrews 4:14; 6:20; John 18:37; Revelation 19:16.

CHAPTER 8: THE MINOR PROPHETS

1. Samuel J. Schultz, *The Old Testament Speaks: A Complete Survey of the Old Testament* (San Francisco: Harper, 2000), 229.

CHAPTER 9: THE GOSPELS AND ACTS

1. Preben Vang and Terry G. Carter, *Telling God's Story: The Biblical Narrative from Beginning to End*, 3rd ed. (Nashville: B&H Academic, 2021), 234.
2. It should be noted that when the word *gospel* appears in all lowercase type, it refers to the good news about Jesus—the salvation message. When the word is capitalized—*Gospel*—if refers to one (or all) of the first four books of the New Testament: Matthew, Mark, Luke, John.
3. Tim Keller, "The Centrality of the Gospel," Redeemer City to City blog, January 1, 2000, https://redeemercitytocity.com/articles-stories/the -centrality-of-the-gospel.

CHAPTER 10: PAUL'S LETTERS TO CHURCHES

1. D. A. Carson and Douglas J. Moo, *An Introduction to the New Testament* (Grand Rapids: Zondervan, 2005), 331.
2. Martin Luther, *Commentary on Romans*, trans. J. Theodore Mueller (Grand Rapids: Kregel, 1976), xiii.
3. Outline adapted from the *NLT Life Application Study Bible, Third Edition*, copyright © 2019 by Tyndale House Publishers, Carol Stream, Illinois 60188. All rights reserved. Used by permission.
4. Outline adapted from the *NLT Life Application Study Bible*.
5. Outline adapted from the *NLT Life Application Study Bible*.

CHAPTER 11: PAUL'S PASTORAL LETTERS

1. Andreas J. Köstenberger, L. Scott Kellum, and Charles L. Quarles, *The Cradle, the Cross, and the Crown: An Introduction to the New Testament* (Nashville: Broadman and Holman Academic, 2016), 717.
2. 1 Timothy 3:1-13; Titus 1:6-9.

CHAPTER 13: REVELATION

1. Stanley J. Grenz, *The Millennial Maze: Sorting Out Evangelical Options* (Downers Grove, IL: IVP Academic, 1992), 202.

CONCLUSION: YOUR COMMITMENT TO GOD'S WORD

1. Brad J. Waggoner, *The Shape of Faith to Come: Spiritual Formation and the Future of Discipleship* (Nashville: Broadman and Holman, 2008), 69.
2. If you are wondering, yes, this philosophical calendar difference between my wife and me is a point of tension in our marriage that she seems to win month after month. I'm also wondering if she reads endnotes. I guess I'll find out.

About the Author

Sam Rainer serves as president of Church Answers and is a cofounder of Rainer Publishing. He is also lead pastor at West Bradenton Baptist Church in Bradenton, Florida. He writes, teaches, speaks, and consults on a variety of church health issues. In addition, Sam cohosts the popular podcasts *Rainer on Leadership* and *EST.church*.

Sam is the author of *Obstacles in the Established Church* and the coauthor of *Essential Church?* He has written hundreds of articles for several publications and is a frequent conference speaker on church health issues.

Sam holds a BS in finance and marketing from the University of South Carolina, an MA in missiology from Southern Seminary, and a PhD in leadership studies from Dallas Baptist University. He resides in Bradenton, Florida, with his wife and four children. The Rainers are also a foster family, so it's likely there are more kids in the house at any given time. They have a dog and a cat that his daughters insisted on keeping.

If you liked this book, you'll want to get involved in

Church Member Equip!

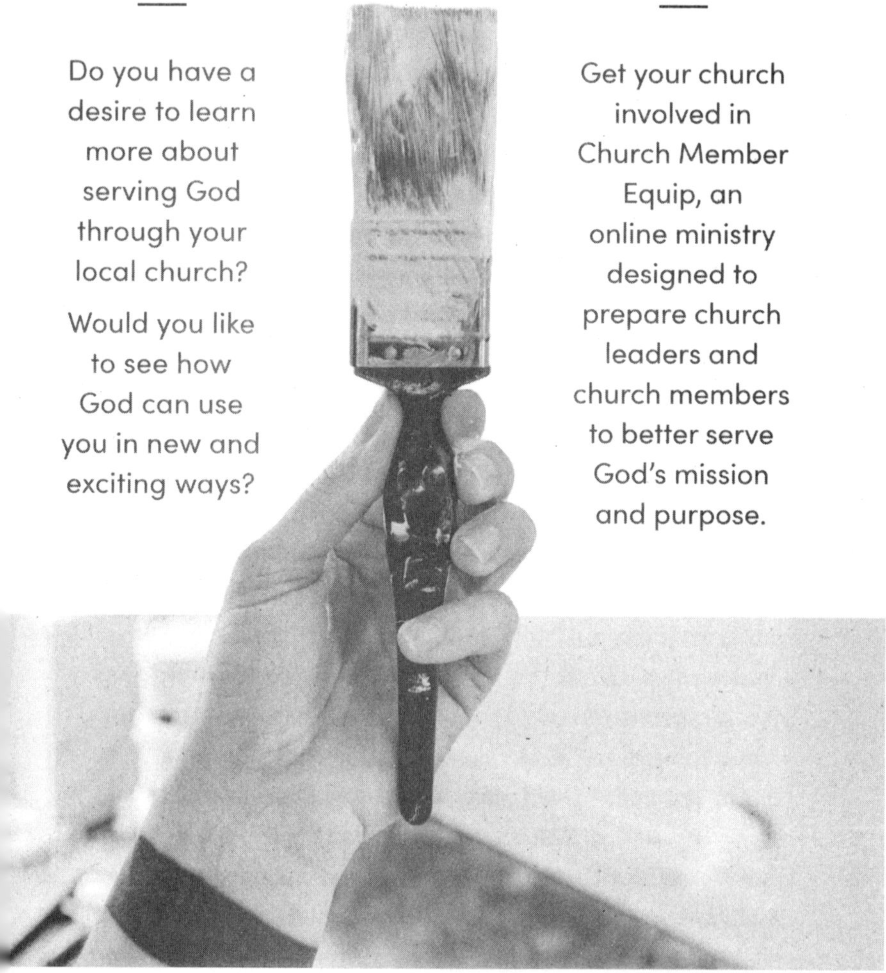

Do you have a desire to learn more about serving God through your local church?

Would you like to see how God can use you in new and exciting ways?

Get your church involved in Church Member Equip, an online ministry designed to prepare church leaders and church members to better serve God's mission and purpose.

Check us out at www.ChurchMemberEquip.com

CHURCH ANSWERS
FEATURING THOM RAINER

CP1749